The Kirkcudbrightshire Companion

D1344165

This book is dedicated to the memory of those
responsible for my Stewartry upbringing:
my father John Irvine Haig Gordon (1916-64);
my mother Nora Gladys Cox (1917-94).

THE KIRKCUDBRIGHTSHIRE COMPANION

Haig Gordon

Galloway Publishing
Kirkcudbright

Published in Scotland
by
Galloway Publishing
The Studio
Gas Lane
Kirkcudbright
Kirkcudbrightshire
DG6 4HX

© 2008 Galloway Publishing

ISBN
Paper-bound
978-0-9553183-3-7

A CIP catalogue record for this book
is available from the British Library.

All rights reserved.
No part of this publication may be reproduced in any form or by
any means – graphic, electronic or mechanical, including photo-
copying, recording, taping or information storage and retrieval
systems – without the prior permission in writing of the publisher.

Printed in Scotland
by Bell and Bain, Glasgow

Contents

Acknowledgements

You may notice that some of the photographs in this book are markedly superior to others. These are the work of Norman Chalmers (yes, the very same one who performs with Jock Tamson's Bairns!). It was a joy to accompany him on his Stewartry photo-shoot, during which no physical obstacle was ever allowed to get in the way of achieving the image he was after. The publisher and I are deeply grateful not only for the splendid pictures he provided but also for his wise guidance on making the most of the other illustrations available to us.

I should also like to thank David Henderson for the aerial photograph of Kirkcudbright on page 84.

For other images I am grateful to the following: Ken Cargill, the Cavendish Laboratory, the Dorothy L Sayers Society, Dumfries and Galloway Council, Felicity and Ian Gelder, the Harbour Cottage Gallery trustees, Wilson Lochhead, Elizabeth McKnight, the National Library of Scotland, National Museums Scotland, the National Trust for Scotland, W A C Smith, J L Stevenson, Mike Tosh and the US Naval Academy. The diagram of a drystane dyke on page 156 first appeared in F Rainsford-Hannay's invaluable *Dry Stone Walling*. The drawing of Hills Tower on page 99 is from *The Fortified House in Scotland* by Nigel Tranter and shows that this great writer was also a considerable artist.

For quotations from authors I am indebted to the following publishers: Abacus (Charles Jennings); William Heinemann and Victor Gollancz (Edwin Muir); Methuen & Co (H V Morton); John Smith & Son (Andrew McCormick).

David Collin was, as ever, extremely helpful, in particular by allowing me a pre-publication look at his splendid *Kirkcudbright Shipping 1300-2005*. Through the kindliness of Andrew and Doris Macdonald I was able to visit the Creetown Heritage Museum during the off-season.

In the early stages of planning this book Barry Smart of Castle Douglas gave me much encouragement and I benefited incalculably from numerous conversations with him.

A final thank-you to Glen Murray of Galloway Publishing. In the preparation of this project I have had the rare good fortune to work with a publisher who knows more about the subject than the author does!

Introduction

You may, if you like, call it Kirkcudbrightshire. But its proper name is The Stewartry of Kirkcudbright. What a delicious mouthful! Not just the Stewartry bit – but also the almost comical mismatch between the spelling of Kirkcudbright and its pronunciation, *Kir-COO-bray*. If you're a stranger in these parts, you'll probably be baffled already. Good. We locals like it that way. It makes us feel rather special, which of course we are.

There used to be other stewartries in Scotland, distant and sometimes unruly areas administered on behalf of the monarchy by a *steward*. The rest have disappeared. Now we are *The* Stewartry. And long may it continue – despite the steady bureaucratic erosion of its separateness.

The Stewartry is one of the two counties that form Galloway, which came into being as a medieval lordship operating more or less independently from a not-quite-fully-formed Scotland. Wigtownshire, to the west, is the other. Stewartry people call it The Shire. Histories and guide-books for this south-west corner of Scotland almost invariably deal with Galloway as a single entity. But we Stewartry folk know that The Shire is alien territory. For one thing, they speak differently in Wigtownshire, with an Irish tinge to their tongue. They get their news from the *Galloway Gazette*; we have the *Galloway News,* though we wish sentimentally that it was still called the *Kirkcudbrightshire Advertiser.* It may make sense, in the long run of history, to generalise about Galloway, but in reality the two counties have separate identities and command unique loyalties.

The Stewartry traditionally extends from the River Cree in the west to the River Nith in the east, with the northern hills around Loch Doon forming a natural frontier with Ayrshire. Those were the boundaries recognised by the Local Government (Scotland) Act 1889 under which the Stewartry of Kirkcudbright County Council came into effect. But subsequent reorganisations of Scotland's local government have blurred those customary borders for administrative convenience.

In 1974 a two-tier system of large Regions and smaller Districts was introduced. The new Stewartry District Council, subsumed within the Dumfries and Galloway Region, appeared in its name to have retained the integrity of our ancient identity. In fact the boundaries of the new jurisdiction had been shrunk to such an extent that, for example, Creetown in the west of the Stewartry was induced into thinking that it was now part of Wigtownshire. In the east, villages as far west as Crocketford and New Abbey were somehow persuaded that their affiliation was to Dumfriesshire.

In 1995 there was yet another reorganisation of local government, this time back to unitary authorities. In the present overbearingly wide-ranging Dumfries and Galloway Council, the dear old Stewartry is reduced to having just an *area committee* – with its frame of reference again confined to the shrunken boundaries of the 1974 farrago.

In the systematic erosion of the Stewartry's cherished identity, bureaucratic planners have not been the only culprits. The Royal Mail must take its share of the blame, with its insistence on the addresses of small places incorporating the name of the nearest big place, even if the latter is in another county. For example, the postal town for New Abbey in *Kirkcudbrightshire* is Dumfries. Inevitably the next step is to start assuming that New Abbey is therefore in *Dumfriesshire.*

Another institution that ought to know better has made this error official. The 'historians' of the National Museums of Scotland have a part of their archive on display in New Abbey. Shamefully, they give as their address there the following misinformation: Shambellie House Museum of Costume, New Abbey, *Dumfriesshire* [my italics].

The whole problem is compounded by the under-educated media who appear to believe that *anywhere* in the whole of the Dumfries and Galloway region (comprising three counties) is in Dumfriesshire. Enough said.

***

This book is in two parts. Pick a Stewartry place and in most cases you'll find it in the alphabetical arrangement of Part One. Entries there may also have cross-references to the thematic chapters of Part Two. It will be obvious from the above rant that the parameters of the book pre-date the 1970s meddling.

Part One

THE PLACES

Anwoth - Twynholm

Anwoth

Samuel Rutherford

This tiny clachan entered national consciousness in the early-seventeenth century through the controversial activities of its Presbyterian minister **Samuel Rutherford** (about 1600-61). He was the leading theorist behind the Covenanters' resistance to the Crown's attempts to impose Episcopalian or 'popish' forms of worship on the Church of Scotland. Rutherford's stance was militant and bitterly unyielding. From his pen came a torrent of books and correspondence in defence of the purity of the Kirk. His most influential publication was *Lex, rex, or, The Law and the Prince* (1644), in which he set out to justify the Covenanters' taking up arms against Charles I.

The highs and lows of Rutherford's career paralleled the ups and downs of the Covenanting cause. He became the minister at Anwoth in 1627 but nine years later, in a crackdown on the extremists, was sentenced to be confined to Aberdeen (today that might still be a punishment). Although eventually he returned to prominence as a preacher, writer and academic, his luck finally ran out in 1660 with the Restoration of Charles II. Rutherford was charged with treason but died before he could be tried.

It is interesting to note that this severe dogmatist, who became known as the Saint of the Covenant, was not entirely a stranger to the sin of lust. Just before he arrived in Anwoth, while he was teaching at the university of Edinburgh, it was 'declared by the principall of the colledge that Mr Samuell Rutherfuird...hes fallin in furnicatioun with Euphame Hamilton, and hes committit ane grit scandle'. He was sacked from his academic post. The Anwoth job was his earthly salvation.

Anwoth
Old Kirk

The now roofless **Anwoth Old Kirk** was brand-new in Rutherford's day. Exactly two hundred years later it was superseded by the adjacent parish kirk, now deconsecrated. For many years the Old Kirk was a place of pilgrimage for Rutherford admirers. The only pilgrims to be seen these days are movie fans on the trail of *The Wicker Man* locations (see Part 2 - The Movie). The film showed pagans dancing round a maypole where Rutherford had once harangued his congregation. The old schoolhouse across the road also featured in the film.

The granite obelisk overlooking Anwoth from the Boreland Hill is the **Rutherford Memorial**, erected in 1842 (and re-built in 1851 after being struck by lightning) 'in admiration of his eminent talents, ministerial faithfulness, and distinguished public labours in the cause of civil and religious liberty'. Below is a Biblical quotation: 'The righteous shall be in everlasting remembrance'.

On an adjacent peak is a **millennium monument** of 2000, commemorating the ministers of the Anwoth parish since the Reformation and those of the combined Anwoth and Girthon parish since 1975. Constructed of granite, whinstone and slate, with a cross on top, it is dedicated to the incumbent at the time of erection, the Rev Austin Erskine.

A short distance to the east on **Trusty's Hill** is the only evidence in this part of Scotland of a Pictish presence. It is easy to spot: what looks at first like the rusty remains of abandoned agricultural machinery is in fact the cage protecting Pictish carvings on two slabs of rock at the entrance to a first- or second-century fort. Archaeologists are unsure of what the Picts were doing here so far from their northern homelands. Some suggest that the carvings may have been the 'calling-card' of a raiding-party, others that they are evidence of Dark Age diplomatic contact between the Picts and the tribes of the south-west. It is likely that we shall never know.

The Pictish symbols should not be confused with later carvings, in particular those of one Billy Cain in June 1955.

The Old Schoolhouse, Anwoth

Auchencairn

The Old Smugglers Inn

The village grew up around the corn mill that was powered by the Hass Burn. Auchencairn Bay had salt-pans, and from the mid-nineteenth century there was a salmon fishery using stake-nets. Periodically through the nineteenth and twentieth centuries, **mining** activities took place: for iron at Auchenleck to the north-west, and for copper and barytes along the Rascarrel and Bar-locco coast to the south. An attempt to mine for coal at Rascarrel was unsuccessful.

During the eighteenth century Auchencairn's economy flourished – and all of it was illegal. **Smuggling** was a major 'industry' right along the northern Solway coast, and nowhere more so than around Auchencairn Bay.

The area had everything required: closeness to the principal staging-post, the Isle of Man; plenty of coves and caves for concealment of goods; and an impoverished population outraged by taxes imposed by a London-based government following the Union of the Parliaments of Scotland and England in 1707. The 'trade' was mainly in tea, tobacco, rum, brandy and wine. There was hardly anyone who was not involved in some way, from humble households to highly organised syndicates. Even the clergy were complicit, though they were less inclined to turn a blind eye on the Sabbath.

Locations associated with the smugglers are all around. On the coast south of Balcary Hill a popular rock from which to watch for incoming cargoes is still called Adam's Chair. On the shore of Balcary Bay, Balcary House (now a hotel) was built complete with cellars, reputedly as the centre of operations for a Manx smuggling company. On the peninsula at the north-east part of Auchencairn Bay the now deserted village of Craigrow was entirely dependent on smuggling. Chief among the smugglers of Craigrow was Johnnie Girr. He prospered so much that he began building a fine house for himself. When during a government crackdown on his business he ran short of cash, he was rescued, it is said, by a bequest from a brother who had fought in the Battle of Bunker Hill in the American War of Independence. When Johnnie's house was completed he called it Bunker Hill.

The most celebrated smugglers' spot is **Hestan Island** at the mouth of Auchencairn Bay. Its rocky coastline offered plenty of hiding-places and look-out points. Rathan Isle in S R Crockett's smuggling yarn *The Raiders* was modelled on Hestan (Crockett often holidayed in Auchencairn – he had relatives here).

However, the island's history of occupation goes back much further. In the twelfth and thirteenth centuries it was controlled by Dundrennan Abbey. The monks used it for fishing and grazing. In the fourteenth century it was an occasional base for Edward Balliol who had a brief career as a puppet Scottish king under the sponsorship of England. The foundations of Balliol's fortified house can still be traced.

From about 1600 onwards the island was in the ownership of the Earls of Nithsdale. During the nineteenth century there was copper mining. According to the 1841 census, three miners were resident on the island, presumably in the cottage that still exists. Between 1909 and 1947 four families, the Starks, the Flemings, the Tweedies and the McWilliams, lived there, grazing their sheep and tending the lighthouse.

In 1947, despite being already beyond retirement age, James Houston moved to the island. He was tough, and had to be. On one occasion he slipped and damaged, possibly even fractured,

Balcary House around 1895

Auchencairn

Hestan Island with stake nets in the foreground

an elbow but treated himself homeopathically. He was 'most reluctant to leave the island' when he was finally persuaded back to the mainland.

The last full-time occupation was by Beryl and John Scott in the late 1950s. Their spartan existence is described in Beryl's *On a Galloway Island* (2003). They built the island's first-ever bathroom, recycling an old tub that had long been in use as a cattle-trough. John was an organ builder. While on the island he built two organs, which were then dismantled and taken section by section on a small boat to the mainland.

The Auchencairn area has attracted the wealthy with a penchant for conspicuous display in housing. South from the village, on the way to Balcary, is **Auchencairn House**, a mansion built in the 1860s for Ivie Mackie, a former Lord Mayor of Manchester. Northeast of the village is **Orchardton House**, a flamboyant Scottish Baronial/English Jacobean mansion of the 1880s constructed around an earlier house. The Orchardton estate was acquired in 1786 by a brother of Sir William Douglas, founder of Castle Douglas.

At one time every Stewartry village had its resident versifier. Auchencairn's star-turn was the blacksmith **Joseph Heughan** (1837-1902). Some of his metalwork is preserved at the Stewartry Museum in Kirkcudbright. His doggerel is less enduring:

> Puir ell-wan' Johnnie canna sleep,
> Since Jeanie's gaed awa',
> The saut tears thro' his winkers dreep,
> His een's like meltin' snaw.
> He's blearie and weary,
> The chiel's gane nearly doylt,
> Wi' mournin' and yearnin',
> His fair physog is spoilt.   (from *The Wooer's Plicht*)

Balmaclellan

OLD MORTALITY
LIVED
17 HERE 68

Balmaclellan flaunts its association with 'Old Mortality', the eighteenth-century stonemason **Robert Paterson** (died 1801) who devoted most of his working life to carving Covenanter memorials for no financial reward and achieved posthumous fame in Sir Walter Scott's *Old Mortality* (1816).

At the front of the kirk the sculptured tableau of man and pony has a plaque stating: 'Old Mortality lived here 1768'. If he *did* live here, his stay was a short one, for the point about Paterson is that his fanatical attachment to the cause led him to abandon his wife and five children, who are the ones who really deserve a statue.

Paterson was from the parish of Hawick in the Borders and learned his trade at Lochmaben in Dumfriesshire. He became a member of the fundamentalist Presbyterian group known as the Cameronians, and was frequently away from home attending gatherings of the sect and caring for the gravestones of the Covenanting 'martyrs'. Around 1758, by which time he was under the total influence of his religious mania, he decided not to return home, though there had been no evidence of marital discord. Successive deputations from his children, pleading with him to come back to them, failed to melt his dogmatic resolve. Realising after about ten years that he was not going to return, his wife Elizabeth brought the family to Balmaclellan where she supported them by running a school. Elizabeth is buried in the kirkyard, but it is her runaway husband who gets the star treatment.

Balmaclellan

The main body of the **parish kirk** was built in 1753, and added to in 1833. The gravestones in the kirkyard include a table stone commemorating the Covenanting 'martyr' Robert Grierson.

The vantage-point at the **war memorial** overlooking the village from the east offers a panoramic view of the Rhinns of Kells, whose names are to be savoured: Millfore, Curleywee, Bennan, Little Millyea, Meikle Millyea, Milldown, Corserine and Meaul.

There is also from here a clear view of the twelfth- or thirteenth-century **motte**, its shape like a perfect upturned pudding, as if deposited there out of a giant baking mould.

Balmaclellan is the kind of small, out-of-the-way place that appeals to urban refugees seeking revivalist rusticity through niche cottage-industries. Such enterprises often fizzle out after the novelty stage. Top prize for longevity goes to the **Clog and Shoe Workshop** which opened in the former village school in the 1970s.

To the north-east of the village, **Barscobe Castle** is misnamed: though it has features associated with fortified tower houses, it is really just a sturdy laird's house of 1648. In the early 1970s restoration began under its then owner Sir Hugh Wontner, Lord Mayor of London in 1973 and at one time head of the Savoy hotel group.

Barscobe Castle

Bargrennan

B eing on the east side of the River Cree, Bargrennan makes it into the Stewartry (just). The diminutive hostelry, the House o' Hill Hotel, is well placed for the Southern Upland Way which passes through here.

Not all the walkers are doing the long-distance path. Some are searching the forestry plantation north-east of the clachan for the **White Cairn**, a burial chamber with passageway dating from around 3000 BC. It is the prime example among a dozen or so similar structures found in the area. During an excavation in 1949 cremated bones were found in what had been a ritual fire-pit, along with about 60 tiny fragments of late-neolithic pottery.

Beeswing

H ow did a wee place originally called Lochend (sensibly enough, given its proximity to Loch Arthur) end up getting such a quaint-sounding change of identity? It is all down to a mid-nineteenth-century racehorse owner who purchased the inn and re-named it after Beeswing, a championship horse that had won 51 races in eight seasons. Just to confuse matters, the kirk, built 1867-8, continued to use the name Lochend and, when a railway served this community, the station was known as Killywhan.

To the south of the village is the **Loch Arthur Community**, run by the Camphill Village Trust for adults with special needs. The 500-acre estate is farmed organically. The products of its creamery, especially the cheese, and of its bakery are much appreciated by local epicures.

Another sweet local name is **Lotus**, which proliferates: Lotus Hill; Lotus House (an early-nineteenth-century mansion within the Loch Arthur estate); and, at one time, Loch Arthur was known as Loch Lotus. The loch was the site of a crannog, an aquatic defensive homestead common in Iron Age Scotland and Ireland.

Loch Arthur

11

Borgue

Borgue folk have aye had a 'guid conceit o thirsels', and that fact is not surprising when you consider that the parish merits several entries in the *Dictionary of the Scots Language*:

Go to Borgue: 'expresses only good-humoured impatience with one who has used ridiculous or trifling arguments in a friendly discussion - arguments to which there was no sensible reply'.

Out of the world and into Borgue: '...meaning that Borgue is a primitive place where anything odd or curious might be found. A native of Borgue took it to mean that in Borgue one would find "rest and peace".'

In the 1790s the New Galloway-born writer Robert Heron alluded to the outsider's view of Borgue folk:

> ...by inhabiting a sort of promontory and divided from neighbours by the sea upon two sides, they were long regarded by other people of this district as sort of peculiar. The families of farmers had been settled there for many generations; they were all mutually related by intermarriages. They looked upon their neighbours with aversion and contempt. A person of singular appearance or manners was commonly said by the people of the adjacent country to be a Borgue Body.

An old bard of the parish had his own angle on this near-incestuous insularity:

Borgue lads delight to marry lasses bonny,
Yet scorn to gang frae hame to seek for ony;
They'd tak a sister o' their ain, by Jove,
Afore they'll through anither parish rove.

The same phenomenon may help to explain the abundance of families with the same surnames:

O famous parish for Browns and Sproats,
The like o't's no' on this side o' John o' Groats

Of all the human oddities produced by Borgue, none was more eccentric than **John Mactaggart** whose *Scottish Gallovidian Encyclopedia* (1824) is one of the strangest books ever published in Scotland, a garrulous gallimaufry of old phrases, legends and scurrilous gossip. Not surprisingly, his native parish comes out of it well:

BORGUE—One of the most singular and celebrated parishes in the south of Scotland, and one too of the very best that is to be found in any country...

There's another Borgue entry:

BORGUE-HINNIE—Borgue honey. This article is of such good quality, that the fame of its excellence spreads far and wide. In London there is a sign, with *Borgue-hinnie for ever*, wrote on it.

Mactaggart (1797-1830) spent his early years at Lennox Plunton on the north-west boundary of Borgue parish. His father was a tenant farmer and, when John was about eight, the family moved to Torrs at the other side of Kirkcudbright Bay.

His career was adventurous but dogged with misfortune. He went to London and started a newspaper, *The London Scotsman*, but it folded after just a few weeks. He then took up engineering, and emigrated to Canada to work on the Rideau Canal linking the River Ottawa with Lake Ontario. Owing to his mother's ill-health, he returned home in 1829, but he too was sick and he died the following year.

When his Galloway book was published, his father is reputed to have said to him: 'John, yer ain family kent ye were a fool, but noo the hale world'll ken'.

13

Borgue

Another Borgue man of letters was the legendary wandering minstrel **William Nicholson** (1783-1849), who is commemorated by a bronze plaque outside Borgue school. Set in Dalbeattie granite, the image is taken from a painting by the Gatehouse of Fleet artist John Faed. It was placed here in 1900 (see Part 2 - The Bards).

Nicholson memorial

Borgue has always been particularly proud of its school, so revered that it was given the name of **Borgue Academy**, a term usually applied only to large secondary schools in towns. Education in the parish was put on a firm footing by Thomas Rainy (born 1731), a cooper's son from Auchenhay farm who made a fortune as a coffee-planter in Dominica. He wanted 'to remedy the defects of his early school discipline owing in some measure to the unskilfulness of the master and partly to the innumerable errors of an early edition of Cole's dictionary...' He insisted also that Latin should be taught, since that was the one compulsory subject for university entrance. The new school premises came into operation in 1803. The schoolhouse was large enough to accommodate boarders, who came from far afield. The present school building was substantially altered in 1911. Its name, sadly, has reverted back to just plain Borgue School.

Borgue's best-known landmark is the **parish kirk**, built in 1814 with later additions towards the end of the century. On its exposed elevation, it was notoriously cold until decent heating was installed. A local wag used to say, 'I would rather roast in Hell than freeze to death in Borgue Kirk'.

Borgue
Parish Kirk

To the east of the village, **Borgue House** stands side by side with Borgue Old House. The former is a mid-nineteenth-century laird's dwelling, while the latter, now a roofless ruin, dates from the late-seventeenth century, though it may have incorporated fabric from an even earlier building.

Borgue Old House was home to **Hugh Blair**, who was the subject of a sensational court case in the 1740s. He was, in the terminology of his times, an 'idiot'. But his mother wanted him to marry and arranged for Nicholas [correct] Mitchell, the daughter of a Kirkcudbright surgeon, to be his wife. His younger brother John, concerned about his inheritance, objected and successfully applied to the court in Edinburgh to have the marriage annulled. The case has been taken up in recent years as an object-lesson in how not to treat the mentally impaired. In *Autism in History: The Case of Hugh Blair of Borgue* (2000), Rab Houston (a social historian) and Uta Frith (a professor of cognitive development) argue that Blair was what we would now call autistic.

Borgue House was acquired in 1931 by **Henry Dalziel** (1868-1935), an outstanding example of a local lad made good. His father was a Borgue cobbler, and Henry himself became apprenticed in that trade. But, after a fight, he left the village under a cloud. That was the making of him.

He learned shorthand and became a journalist, eventually specialising in reporting the House of Commons. He soon swapped the press gallery for the chamber itself, becoming Liberal MP for Kirkcaldy at the age of 24. Meanwhile, his journalistic interests turned to the business side and he grew into a newspaper magnate. Along the way he acquired a knighthood, and in 1921 was created Lord Dalziel, after which he sold his publishing empire and became semi-retired.

After buying the Borgue House estate, he developed a passion for breeding Clydesdale horses, and had numerous successes at the Highland Show with mares such as Belle o' Borgue, Rose o' Borgue, Charm o' Borgue, Queen o' Borgue and Bess o' Borgue.

His wife died in 1935, and, heartbroken, he followed her three weeks later. He is remembered every year at the local flower show, when the Lord Dalziel Cup is presented for 'Most Outstanding Exhibit in the Cut Flower Section'. During his lifetime he contributed financially to the amenities of the parish. Unfortunately, he did not continue his generosity posthumously: he died intestate and, since he was childless, his vast wealth went straight to the Exchequer. 'It is said,' according to Borgue's indefatigable historian Adam Gray, 'that it paid off one day's interest of the National Debt'.

Another Borgue lad who accumulated wealth and entered Parliament was farmer's son **Samuel Smith** (1836-1906). He was schooled at both Borgue and Kirkcudbright, and then studied classics at Edinburgh University. After graduating, he abandoned his scholarly interests and trained as a cotton broker in Liverpool. It was the cotton industry that made him wealthy. When he started to give away money to good causes, his philanthropic instincts were distinctly pious: the Young Men's Christian Association and the temperance movement were amongst his favourite recipients. A Borgue bequest was earmarked for 'Bible Knowledge'. Although he was a frequent visitor to Borgue, his life remained centred on Liverpool. He became an MP for the city in 1882, and, after losing his seat through redistribution, he spent a decade as MP for Flintshire, not far away in north Wales. There is a memorial to him in Liverpool's Sefton Park.

Borgue has a connection with the infamous Charge of the Light Brigade in 1854, a disastrous Crimean War cavalry attack against the Russians in which one third of the British perished. **Sir William Gordon** (1830-1906) was one of the few officers to survive, though he sustained many injuries. His batman, another Borgue native by the name of John Wilson, was less fortunate – he was killed and is buried in Borgue kirkyard. Sir William continued his military career, including the response to the Indian Mutiny, and finally retired back to Borgue in 1864. The family home, now demolished, was within the Earlston estate due north of the village. Perhaps because he had come so close to an early appointment with his Maker, Sir William spent much of his retirement in the service of the Kirk. In the year of his death, the parish magazine paid tribute:

> If he was the acknowledged head of the Parish, he was every whit as much its heart. While there was no bigotry about his Churchmanship, few laymen could equal him in his observance of the Lord's day in the house of God.

Lady Gordon survived him by a couple of decades, and made her own contribution to uplifting the spirits of the parish by founding a temperance coffee-house.

Bridge of Dee

Two bridges, actually. The whinstone and granite **Old Bridge of Dee**, at the heart of the village, dates from the early-eighteenth century. This was part of the main route across Galloway until it was replaced around 1825 by a new bridge on the toll road from Dumfries to Portpatrick. This replacement structure is now called **Threave Bridge**. It was widened in 1986, being built outwards to the south. The cladding for the new southern elevation came from the original masonry. At the same time the bridge was made straighter than it was at first.

The odd-looking little tin hut on the main street of Bridge of Dee is the **Mission Hall**, an outpost of Balmaghie parish kirk. It was built in 1897, having been financed by public subscription.

The tin-hut kirk

Cargenbridge

Another Stewartry place absorbed into the Dumfries sprawl, and now, at first glance, little more than a housing estate and a chemical works (started during the Second World War). You get a flavour of modern Cargenbridge from an architectural guide's summary of its late-1950s primary school: an 'assemblage of flat-roofed boxes'.

But the Cargenbridge area is surprisingly beautiful. A stroll along Carruchan Beeches between the Dalbeattie and New Abbey main roads is an eye-opener and the numerous mansion-houses in the area are redolent of more elegant times. **Dalskairth**, on the main road to Dalbeattie, originated in the early 1700s but has been much altered since. To the south the late-eighteenth-century **Mabie House** is now a hotel.

The most interesting mansion, opposite Dalskairth and now a retirement home, is **Goldielea**, a grand creation of the late-eighteenth century. It got its name from the original owner Colonel Goldie and his wife whose maiden name was Leigh. The house has associations with the poet Robert Burns. His friend Maria Riddell - a beauty who was painted by Sir Thomas Lawrence - moved into it in 1792 along with her feckless husband Walter. He too made use of his wife's maiden name, re-naming the estate Woodley Park. But after a few years Colonel Goldie re-possessed the house, Walter Riddell having failed to raise sufficient cash for the final payment.

Goldielea and the viaduct

Despite a period of estrangement after a party at which Burns drank too much and allegedly misbehaved, the friendship between the poet and Maria was extremely close. She was with him shortly before he died, and wrote in a memoir: 'I was struck with his appearance on entering the room. The stamp of death was imprinted on his features. He seemed already touching the brink of eternity.'

Burns disliked Walter, and said so in verse:

> So vile was poor Wat, such a miscreant slave
> That the worms even damn'd him when laid in the grave.
> 'In his skull there's a famine!' a starved reptile cries;
> 'And his heart, it is poison!' another replies.

The house has a stunning backdrop: the Grade A-listed **Goldielea Viaduct**, completed in 1859 for the Dumfries to Castle Douglas railway but disused since the 'Beeching Axe' of the mid-1960s. In 2005 Scottish Natural Heritage excitedly announced the discovery of 50,000 specimens of common wintergreen on the viaduct, and also of a colony of bats, which are legally protected. Steam railway enthusiasts groaned.

In the nineteenth century Cargenbridge was home to an outstanding example of the Victorian upper-class gentleman-scholar: the eclectic writer, antiquarian and amateur scientist **Patrick Dudgeon** (1817-1895). Mineralogy was the greatest of his many passions. His collection of 3,538 specimens remains a significant part of the Scottish national archive. He was also a meteorologist, and dabbled in many other fields, including history and linguistics. He wrote *The Origin of Surnames*; *The Macs of Galloway*; and a Scots glossary for the works of his friend, the Stewartry novelist S R Crockett. Before his sudden death he had been working on a dictionary demonstrating the connections between Galloway Scots and Anglo-Saxon, but had got only as far as D.

Patrick Dudgeon

Dudgeon was an early enthusiast for what we now term 'green' burials, and left behind strict instructions for his 'earth to earth' interment, which the *Dumfries & Galloway Standard* described as:

> ...the body being placed in a wicker coffin in order to hasten decomposition, in the interests of public health, where the graveyard is situated amid a crowded population. To give the effect as far as possible to the wish of the deceased in this respect the coffin was made (by the joiners

> on the estate) of only light wood, unlined and perforated, so
> as to leave the body open to the action of the air...

Dudgeon was an East Lothian man who had worked in China for some years. He and his wife had friends on the Stewartry coast and, through visiting them, became so enamoured of the area that they decided to settle here. They bought the Cargen estate and, in the early 1870s, had a new house built in the Scottish Baronial style. The house is now a ruin.

Given the recent erosion in this area of its original west-of-the-Nith Stewartry identity, it is worth emphasising - lest these adopted Doonhamers forget - that Dudgeon's public service was for the *Stewartry*, and that from 1908 till 1932 his son, Colonel R F Dudgeon, was Lord Lieutenant of the *Stewartry*.

A short distance to the west of Cargen House is **St Queran's Well**, whose water has long been reputed to have healing qualities. Queran was an Irish saint of the ninth century. Traditionally offerings were placed in the well or hung around it in the form of ribbons. The well was an obvious target of Patrick Dudgeon's antiquarian curiosity, and in the 1870s he had it cleaned out, revealing hundreds of old coins dating as far back as the sixteenth century. Around the start of the twentieth century, a writer observed:

> ...from the number of people who still visit the well, particularly on a fine Sunday afternoon, Mr Dudgeon was inclined to think that the curative powers of the water are, by a few, not yet altogether disbelieved in.

In the twenty-first century, according to the local community council, 'the tradition of leaving small mementos continues and you will see pieces of rag and other similar articles on bushes nearby'.

St Queran's Well   'Offerings' are still left

Carsethorn

According to an early-twentieth-century guide-book author, 'the village itself does not provide matter for a long discourse'. But, before the coming of the railways, when shipping was the principal means of transport for the Stewartry, Carsethorn – or 'The Carse', as it is more informally known - was a significant port.

The name of the present **Steamboat Inn** is a reminder of this maritime past. The village's position at the mouth of the River Nith meant that it developed in particular as a harbour for the town of Dumfries which was too far up-stream to have a viable quayside of its own.

Schooners at Carsethorn - late 19th century

There is still evidence of the wooden **pier** that was constructed in 1840 to link the shore with the sea channel. Its most regular user was the Liverpool Steam Packet Company.

However, Carsethorn's history as a harbour goes much further back. It is first mentioned in this respect in 1562 when a ship was recorded as loading for La Rochelle and Bordeaux. Its return cargo of wine would have been keenly anticipated. So important to Dumfries was Carsethorn that in the 1660s the town's merchants paid for the two locations to be linked by a thirteen-mile cobbled road suitable for wagons.

For tens of thousands of Stewartry folk, Carsethorn represented the heartache of **emigration** in a desperate attempt to find an economically viable way of life. The outflow of people began in the middle of the eighteenth century when agricultural 'improvements' rendered them redundant. One particular departure is now commemorated by an information plaque in the garden of the Steamboat Inn. On May 1, 1775, sixty-six people – ranging in age from 57 years to four months – left on board the

Carsethorn

Ruins of the pier at Carsethorn with Criffel in the background.

Lovely Nelly. Their final destination was St John's Island in North America. Mass emigration through Carsethorn continued well into the nineteenth century. In 1850 alone, it is said, 10,000 left for North America, 7000 for Australia and 4000 for New Zealand.

Carsethorn was also the fateful place of departure in 1760 for **John Paul Jones**, the buccaneer who ended up as an American naval hero (see Part 2 - The Pirate). From his home at nearby Arbigland he had often come here to play among the boats and dream of a life at sea. At the age of just 13, he finally boarded a ship for real, crossing the Solway to Whitehaven to join a merchant ship as an apprentice, the start of an extraordinary career.

Some of those who bade farewell to their native land from Carsethorn had little choice in the matter. **Convicts** sentenced to transportation were marched here from their cells in Dumfries and kept in barracks awaiting shipment into a punitive exile at the other end of the world.

Haaf-net fishing was once a more common sight in the waters around Carsethorn. 'Haaf' comes from Norse and means 'open sea'. Haaf-netters work in teams of about eight. They wade out into the sea, often up to chest level, dragging a huge net on a wooden frame about eighteen feet long. It is a method of fishing that is unique to the Solway, on both the English and Scottish sides.

Haaf-net fishing in the Solway

Carsluith

The village, overlooking Wigtown Bay, used to lie along the main A75, but is now by-passed. Travellers, however, still get a good view of its **castle**, built in the 1560s (on the site of an earlier structure) for the Brouns of Carsluith. This was the birthplace of Gilbert Broun, the last abbot of Sweetheart Abbey, who was eventually sent into exile in the early 1600s as punishment for trying to stop the abbey being closed down by the new Reformed Kirk (see New Abbey).

Carsluith Castle

Like its larger neighbour Creetown, Carsluith has a history of **granite quarrying**. High up behind the village, beyond the farm of Kirkmabreck, are the disused Fell and Silver Grey quarries. These were active from the 1840s and operations did not finally end until 1970. The site now looks as if the last workers just walked away. Massive amounts of extracted granite lie all around, along with the rusty remains of machinery and of the railway that took supplies to the wharf on Wigtown Bay.

In a secluded hollow below the quarries is the ancient **Kirkmabreck kirkyard**. The medieval kirk is now not much more than a pile of rubble. It was abandoned in the mid-seventeenth century in favour of Creetown. The most prominent memorial in Kirkmabreck kirkyard is to **Thomas Brown** (1778-1820), a professor of moral philosophy at Edinburgh University who also fancied himself as a poet. He was the thirteenth child of the Kirkmabreck minister. When he was still very young, his father died and the family moved to Edinburgh. He went to live with an uncle in London and attended school there. Returning to Edinburgh, he spent the rest of his short life locked in arcane metaphysical disputes with fellow philosophers. His enemies described him as 'affected' and 'feminine'. As his health declined, he once again went to London in search of a cure, but did not survive. At his own request, he was buried beside his parents at Kirkmabreck.

Carsluith

Kirkdale House

The local granite was used for the construction in 1787-8 of **Kirkdale House** to the south-east of Carsluith. This was a prestigious project commissioned by Sir Samuel Hannay, a Galloway laird who made a second fortune as a merchant in London. He hired the most fashionable architects of the day, the firm run by the two famous Adam brothers, Robert and James. Following a fire in 1893, the interior was reconstructed in a neo-Jacobean style inconsistent with the Adam exterior.

The Egyptian-style Kirkdale bridge was built at the same time, though the full grandiosity of the Adam design was never quite implemented. The Adams may also have had a hand in the Hannay family mausoleum built in the grounds of a ruined medieval parish kirk behind the big house.

Something a great deal older lies to the north of Kirkdale. This is the pair of prehistoric burial chambers known as **Cairnholy** I and II. They are dated at about 3000 BC. Our more recent ancestors had no notion of conservation and over the years much of the

Cairnholy I

Cairnholy II

stonework has been purloined for the building of drystane-dykes. So what were covered chambers are now open to the elements. Virtually nothing is known about the people who buried their leaders here, but a few of their artefacts have been found, most notably a fragment of a ceremonial axe made of green jadeite from, it is believed, the Alps.

On the shore below Kirkdale is an old smugglers' haunt called (after the character in Walter Scott's *Guy Mannering*) **Dirk Hatteraick's Cave**. Inside there are indentations in the rock for the storage of contraband, and even a recess where a smuggler on guard duty might have rested.

Access to the cave is difficult and dangerous. The Rev C H Dick reported on his own visit in his *Highways and Byways in Galloway and Carrick* (1916). He did not enjoy the experience: 'The cave…is not to be recommended as a health resort, and I should not advise any tramp of my acquaintance to seek a lodging here'. He also describes in considerable detail how Walter Scott's cave differs from the real thing.

Fanciful image of Dirk Hatteraick's Cave
from the Collected Works of Sir Walter Scott

Carsluith

Slightly to the east of Kirkdale House, in an elevated position, is the sixteenth-century **Barholm Castle**. This was in a ruinous state until restored and turned into a four-storey family home. In 2005 the work received a commendation award from the Glasgow Institute of Architects.

Barholm Castle

Visitors to Carsluith today are led by the nose towards the appetising aromas of the **Galloway Smokehouse**. This was established in the late 1960s and taken over in 1985 by Allan Watson. Originally from Nottingham, Allan discovered the delights of smoking food while employed in the Falklands. The islands have an abundance of sea-trout and, having tried every other method of cooking, Allan started to experiment with smoking.

In the early days of the smokehouse there was no farmed salmon. The business was located here to take advantage of the catches from the River Creel/ Wigtown Bay stake-nets. But the numbers of wild salmon are now drastically reduced and, while a couple of the Cree nets remain in use, it is now largely from the marine farms of Scotland that the fish are sourced.

The Galloway Smokehouse adds its own unique flavour by smoking in kilns burning sawdust from old whisky barrels. The sawdust is 'a by-product from a nearby cooperage where whisky barrels are refurbished. The barrel bands are taken off and all the joints are re-planed to give a watertight seal. These shavings impregnated with whisky are burnt in the smokers to give the rich strength of taste to all our products'.

This stretch of coastal road was famously eulogised by the Dumfriesshire-born writer **Thomas Carlyle** (1795-1881) in conversation with Queen Victoria. He told her that 'there was no finer or more beautiful drive in her kingdom than the one round the shore of the Stewartry by Gatehouse of Fleet'. His keenness to impress his opinion upon Her Majesty led to a comic incident, as reported by his fellow writer John Ruskin: '...he got so absorbed in his subject that, in drawing his chair closer to the Queen, he at last became aware he had fixed it on her dress, and that she could not move till he withdrew it!'

Carsphairn

The most northerly, most extensive and least populated of the four parishes that make up the Glenkens (the others being Dalry, Balmaclellan and Kells), Carsphairn has for centuries been a place of refreshment on the north-south route between Ayrshire and Galloway. The other route is to the west via Newton Stewart. In the early-nineteenth century, whenever the circuit judge Lord Cockburn was called to the south-west, he preferred to take the Carsphairn way:

> It is all rich in extensive inland views, bounded and varied, not by wide plains which because they are high above the sea are said to be hills, but by real, plainly marked, sticking-up mountains. There are a great many beautiful places, and the whole country is alive with streams. I am not sure that I have seen any better specimen of our Southern Highlands.

The village is spectacularly set between the hill range known as the Rhinns of Kells to the west and the louring mass of Cairnsmore of Carsphairn to the north-east.

To avoid confusion over the Stewartry's Cairnsmores, help is on hand:

> There's Cairnsmore of Fleet,
>   And there's Cairnsmore of Dee;
> But Cairnsmore of Carsphairn's
>   The highest of the three.

The present **kirk** dates from 1815. It is one of the few in Scotland still to have a central communion table of the type introduced at the Reformation. Carsphairn was created a parish in its own right in 1640. The application for parochial status said that the then kirk 'lyes in a desolat wilderness containing 500 Communicants', and that it had been built at the expense of 'some gentleman out of love for the souls of barbarous and ignorant people, who have hitherto been without knowledge of God, their children un-baptised, their dead unburied'.

Carsphairn was zealous for the Covenanters' cause in the nasty religious civil war that preoccupied Scotland for more than half of the seventeenth century. The spirited defiance of the au-thorities by the Rev John Semple is commemorated by a plaque inside the kirk. One of Semple's successors was suspected by the congregation of being a government sympathiser and was duly shot dead in the manse.

The **Carsphairn Heritage Centre**, built on the site of a former filling-station at the north end of the village, was opened in 1992.

Across the road from the Heritage Centre is **Lagwyne Village Hall**.The name Lagwyne (or Lag-wine) refers to the nearby ruins of a mock-castle built in the 1750s by James McAdam, father of the man who revolutionised road surfacing, **John Loudon McAdam**. Although he was really an Ayrshireman, John Loudon is claimed by Carsphairn; there is a memorial plaque in the kirk. He might have lived for longer in Car-sphairn if Lagwyne had not been burned down in 1762 when he was six years old. James Boswell, the biographer of Dr Samuel Johnson, had recently visited the McAdam home, and a corre-spondent broke the news to him:

> …the house at Lagwine, which afforded you a hospitable retreat on your road to Galloway was burned to ashes about ten days ago. With great difficulty the children's lives were preserved by their leaping naked out of windows two storeys high. Not a single paper nor piece of furniture could be saved from the flames. It is a prodigious loss to the wor-thy gentleman, particularly as his bills and rights of his es-tate are all destroyed.

To the north-east, beyond Cairnsmore of Carsphairn, is the **Windy Standard Wind Farm**, taking its apt name from the hill where it is located. It is one of Scotland's largest wind-farms. The thirty-six turbines became operational in 1996, and are said to be capable of producing enough electricity for 12,800 average-sized homes.

Windy Standard Wind Farm is not a first for 'green' energy pro-duction in the area. Since the 1930s Carsphairn's waterways have been integral to the supply system for the **Galloway Water Power**

Scheme (see Part 2 - The Hydro). The 'green' and 'water' themes around Carsphairn come together in a spot to the north of the village known as the **Green Well of Scotland**, about which there is no shortage of unlikely legends.

The area around Carsphairn abounds in prehistoric remains, like the **stone circle** at Holm of Daltallochan north-west of the village. Close to this spot are intriguing remains of more recent vintage: the deserted village of **Woodhead**, which grew up to accommodate the lead-miners working here between 1838 and the 1870s. The lead was taken to the Ayrshire coast and shipped to Liverpool. At its zenith there was a population of over 300, a church, a school and a library. In 1844 Lord Cockburn witnessed developments at Woodhead and was approving: 'The lately detected lead-mines near Carsphairn, instead of marring, to my taste improve the scene, and even increase its wildness. It looks like a colony of solitary strangers who were trying to discover subterranean treasures in a remote land.'

C H Dick, author of *Highways and Byways in Galloway and Carrick,* visiting Woodhead when it was already abandoned, noted that 'the schoolhouse has been turned into a summer lodging by a family who must surely share the tastes of the Silverado Squatters' [a reference to Robert Louis Stevenson's account of living in a former mining camp in California].

A short distance from the village, on the road to Moniaive, is **Knockgray**, home of the Victorian man of letters Alexander Clark Kennedy. In childhood he was a precocious ornithologist and at the age of sixteen, using 'An Eton Boy' as his pen-name, he published *The Birds of Berkshire and Buckinghamshire*.

Despite the anglicising effects of an Eton education, he retained a sentimental attachment to his homeland. He was the author of *Robert the Bruce, a Poem Historical and Romantic* (1884), a work in the manner of Sir Walter Scott that comes with extensive footnotes on the history and natural history of the Stewartry. Clark Kennedy also made embarrassing attempts to write verse in Galloway Scots:

> There canna be a bonnier lan',
> There canna be a fairer!
> Romance an' beauty, han' in han',
> Combine to mak' thee rarer.
> Nae brichter leas beyon' the seas
> My heart frae thee shall sever;
> My latest lays shall sing thy praise,
> Here's 'Galloway for ever!'

Castle Douglas

S o where, you might well ask, is the *castle* in Castle Douglas? The answer is simple: there isn't one. But the town's founder, who attached his surname to his creation, liked to associate himself with the idea of a castle as a status-symbol. He fancied himself to be descended from the Douglas family who built nearby Threave Castle in the fourteenth century; and eventually he did build himself a mock-castle at Gelston, south-east of the town.

William Douglas (1745-1809) was the son of a small-time farmer at Penninghame in Wigtownshire and began his working life as a pedlar. His aspirations went far beyond his native Galloway. He moved to Glasgow and later to London, and grew rich as a merchant trading - not always respectably - with the colonies. By the 1780s he was ready to return home and lavish his wealth on turning himself into a grand laird. His first acquisition was an estate near his birthplace, which he developed into a town which he called Newton Douglas, now Newton Stewart.

His next opportunity came in 1789 when the local landowner who had been developing the area around Carlingwark Loch was overwhelmed by financial difficulties. In 1765 Alexander Gordon of Culvennan partially drained the loch for access to a limey clay known as **marle**, which was considered to be an excellent fertiliser. He created a canal linking the loch with the River Dee, to transport the marle to the surrounding farmers. The enterprise created much-needed employment and seemed full of promise. By the early 1790s the tiny waterside clachan of Causewayend or Carlingwark had grown to accommodate over 600 people.

After a while, however, the fertiliser ceased to have its original effect (through over-use) and the market for marle collapsed. William Douglas grabbed the opportunity and in 1789 bought the ailing Gordon estate, and proceeded to build the town we now know as Castle Douglas. In 1792 it became a burgh of barony.

Sir William Douglas

The town plan was laid out in the rectilinear fashion of the time, three parallel principal streets, King Street, Queen Street and Cotton Street, intersected at regular intervals by more streets, including, at the point nearest the loch, one called Marle Street. The name of Cotton Street is indicative of the industry which William Douglas now set about trying to establish, with only limited success. It never survived the invention of the power loom, that required either a fast-flowing river or a nearby source of coal for generating steam.

The new town, described by the writer S R Crockett (who lived during his teens at 106 Cotton Street) as 'built at the foot of a hill and ever since running a race up it', flourished as a mercantile centre, but Douglas was still not satisfied. He had the wealth, but not yet the social status he craved. He lobbied strenuously and at last, in 1801, he received a baronetcy. However, *Sir* William was still not content: he wanted to become Lord Douglas. He allocated a budget of £30,000 (a huge sum in those days) for the purchase of the hard-up Lord Kirkcudbright's title and for the bribes needed to have the sale ratified. But his efforts at further elevation had still not borne fruit when he died, a childless bachelor, in 1809. His grand Egyptian-style mausoleum is to the south of the loch at Kelton, down the road from his home at Gelston.

Though Kirkcudbright is the Stewartry's capital *de jure*, modern Castle Douglas can fairly claim the status *de facto*. While off-the-beaten-track Kirkcudbright retains its importance as a legal and administrative centre, Castle Douglas, with its pivotal position on the road network, is the county's **market town** and commercial hub. This role steadily evolved throughout the nineteenth century. Market Hill at the top of King Street is where open-air livestock sales were conducted, the first recorded one being in 1819. Later

Castle Douglas

King Street with the Clock Tower

the town council built a covered mart, which was subsequently leased to Thomas Wallet. The distinctive octagonal Wallets Mart building of today, east from Market Hill, was built around 1900. Other farming-related service businesses sprang up, most notably, along Cotton Street, Wallace's Foundry, a hothouse of engineering ingenuity, and Derby's Mill where they made the famous 'dairy cakes', winter feed of cereals, proteins, minerals and vitamins for cows.

The main thoroughfare, **King Street**, one of the finest and most concentrated shopping highways in the land, reflects Castle Douglas's mercantile vitality from the mid-nineteenth century onwards. Its outstanding buildings, appropriately, are the banks - like the Royal (formerly the National) Bank of Scotland, flamboyantly built in 1864 of Dalbeattie granite. Although businesses come and go, a remarkable number of those in Castle Douglas have been continuous since the 1800s.

Of the town's civic buildings, the emblematic **Clock Tower** on King Street is not quite as old as it may look. The original Town House with tower and cupola, built by Sir William Douglas, was destroyed by fire in 1892. Forty years later its replacement met the same fate. The present version was completed in 1935. Round the corner in St Andrew Street, the **Town Hall** was completed in 1863. At the northern end of King Street, the **library** of 1904 was an Andrew Carnegie benefaction; the **art gallery** was added on in 1938.

What is now the **parish kirk** in Queen Street is dedicated to St Ringan, an alternative version of St Ninian. Since the first part of it was built in 1801, it has served no less than five different denominations: Relief, Reformed Presbyterian, Free, United Free and now mainstream Church of Scotland. If it seems like an architectural hotch-potch, that's because it is: over the years each denomination made its own adaptation.

In St Andrew Street the Scottish Episcopalians stick to plain St Ninian for the name of their church, which was built in the 1850s for the navvies working on the construction of the railway. A long-maturing bequest from the former owner of the Threave estate enabled the church to add on the **Gordon Memorial Hall** (2001) with such a generosity of traditional materials that it could be taken as much older than it actually is. Round the corner in Lochside Road the former parish kirk of St Andrew was converted into the **Lochside Theatre** in the 1990s.

The Carlingwark Cauldron

Although essentially a 'new town', the history of the Castle Douglas area is more complex than it first appears. Its antiquity centres on Carlingwark Loch at the bottom end of the town. It was the mid-eighteenth-century draining of the loch for marle that first revealed much of the evidence. It was discovered that what is now known as Ash Island had been an Iron Age **crannog**, an artificial island-home built on oak piles sunk into the mud. It was connected to the mainland by a causeway – hence the area's medieval name Causewayend, later Carlingwark.

Another stunning discovery was made by fishermen in the 1860s. They dredged up from the loch-bed a large bronze pot, now known as the **Carlingwark Cauldron** and in the care of the National Museums of Scotland. Dated at between 80 and 200 AD, it may have been used at feasts given by the tribal leadership and then later dumped in the loch as an offering to the gods. It contained about one hundred objects: tools, weapons, craftwork and, most interestingly, some Roman objects. The Romans had a military base just a few miles north-west of here at Glenlochar.

Castle Douglas

In 2002 Castle Douglas began to be marketed to tourists as **The Food Town**. After Wigtown in western Galloway became 'The Book Town' and Kirkcudbright re-defined itself as 'The Artists' Town', Castle Douglas may have felt naked without a designation of its own. Though it has a fine array of butchers and bakers, there is no particular reason why Castle Douglas should claim such a status ahead of any number of similar towns in Scotland. Castle Douglas should take pride in what it is; misleading marketing will do it no good. Two years later, the town was embroiled in a controversy over food of a less special kind: should Tesco be given planning permission to build on a site where until 1965 steam trains stopped at the town? The row raged for a whole year, after which – fairly predictably – the supermarket giant won its case. In 2006 The Food Town became The Tesco Town – or, to be more precise, Just Another Tesco Town.

A couple of miles west of the town is **Threave Castle**, one of the most impressive strongholds of its type in Scotland. It was built about 1370-80 for Archibald The Grim, later Earl of Douglas. The 'Grim' was a reference to his countenance when fighting. In 1369 the King appointed him Lord of Galloway, with a brief to keep the unruly south-westerns between the Nith and the Cree in check. Because of his commitments elsewhere, he employed a steward to act on his behalf – hence 'the stewartry'.

The castle was an ostentatious display of both military might and social status. Its situation on an islet in the River Dee gave it a natural line of defence. The island had ample space for workshops and for the grazing of livestock. It could therefore function as a

Threave Castle

Threave House

self-sufficient community in time of siege. In 1455, by which time the 'Black Douglas' dynasty had become over-mighty for the Crown, Threave came under a three-month siege by King James II.

Three and a half centuries later the castle was still in use – as a prison for French captives from the Napoleonic Wars. Its current roofless state owes more to subsequent scavenging by stone-masons than to enemy action.

Threave Garden, south of the town, is a National Trust for Scotland property where most of the gardeners are students at the Trust's School of Practical Gardening, begun in 1959. The garden is renowned for, among other things, its two hundred varieties of daffodils.

The Threave estate was acquired in 1867 by William Gordon, a Liverpool businessman, and it was he who had Threave House built (1872) in the Scots Baronial style. Major Alan Gordon handed over the property to the Trust in 1948, though he was allowed to continue using the house as a shooting-lodge until his death in 1958.

In 2002 the house was refurbished to look as it did in the 1930s. The Gatehouse of Fleet artist John Faed's great rural narrative painting, *The Wappenschaw* (1863), was brought from the NTS headquarters in Edinburgh and given pride of place in the house. In 1866 when the picture was shown at the Royal Academy in London, it was described by one critic as the best in the exhibition.

Caulkerbush

Hardly a village at all, just a focus for the parish of Southwick. The **kirk**, completed in 1891, is charming in its sylvan setting. It might well have been the usual Victorian Gothic in style – instead its features hark back to pre-Reformation Romanesque. The incumbent of Southwick Hall, Sir Mark McTaggart Stewart, was tired of the long round-trip to Colvend kirk, so he commissioned this one. The ruins of the original medieval kirk are due west in the green tranquillity of Southwick kirkyard.

Much of the traffic through Caulkerbush is heading for the Royal Society for the Protection of Birds reserve at **Mersehead**. The reserve encompasses most of the favourite avian habitats: wet meadows, saltmarsh, arable farmland, woodland, mudflats and sand dunes. It was once a working farm – now the husbandry serves as a demonstration-model of wildlife-friendly practices for farmers and landowners in general. Autumn is the busiest season, when huge flocks of barnacle geese arrive from the Arctic along with thousands of ducks, such as teals, wigeons and pintails, from northern Europe. Rare natterjack toads have been successfully introduced to the sand dunes; their 'dusk chorus' is a feature of the spring at Mersehead.

Clarebrand

In the first half of the nineteenth century Clarebrand rejoiced in the presence of a versifying grocer, **Samuel Wilson** (1784-1863). 'Mr Wilson from his youth was literarily inclined, and often courted the Muse', according to the editor of *The Bards of Galloway*. His song, 'May o' Craignair', was particularly popular:

> Saw ye my true-love on yon misty mountain,
> > Or down the dark glen was he chasing the deer,
> Or heard ye his staghounds on Raeberry hunting?
> > He promised ere now to ha'e met wi' me here.
> But why beats my heart as the leaves rustle o'er me!
> > Ah, why heaves my bosom the sigh o' despair!
> Ye maids o' the Solway my laddie restore me,
> > Entice him nae langer frae May o' Craignair.

Clarebrand also had for a while a bardic blacksmith, **John Gerrond** (1765-1832), who styled himself 'The Galloway Poet'. Gerrond was also a poacher and prodigious drinker, propensities that detracted from any success he had in business. He was born in the parish of Kirkpatrick Durham and in 1776 moved to Causeway-end (the progenitor of Castle Douglas) where he learned black-smithing. He opened his smithy at Clarebrand in 1783. This did not prosper. He and his wife moved to Dumfries, but shortly afterwards he left her for seven years to wander around America. More businesses floundered after his return, and he descended into being a kind of pedlar specialising in making anvil hammers. His first book of poems came out in 1802

He was described by Alexander Trotter in *East Galloway Sketches* as:

> ...exceedingly vain of his personal appearance, and kept a looking-glass and a basin and towel in his smithy. He boasted of his fine legs and 'pasters', as he called his ankles, and, when he could afford it, dressed in plush knee breeches, a ruffled shirt, and silver buckles on his shoes. In his latter days he had to dispense with the ruffles and plush, and substitute clogs for shoes.

Gerrond was loathed by John Mactaggart who dismissed him in *The Scottish Gallovidian Encyclopedia* as a 'gow' [fool] and his published work as 'stuff he termed poems; shameless trash...' Gerrond, on the other hand, compared himself to Burns, but today he is almost entirely forgotten.

Colvend

Tiny Colvend, with its charming village hall of 1933, gives its name to the scenic stretch of coast from Castlehill Point eastwards to Portling. The rocky, indented Colvend coast had its uses in the era of smuggling – now it provides for the innocent pleasures of bird-watching and cliff-top walking with stunning views across the Solway Firth to the hills of the Lake District.

In 2005 a visitor centre was opened in the village under the title 'Explore the Secret Coast'. Clearly, if the marketing is successful, the coast will be a secret no more.

Colvend **kirk**, built 1910-11, is closer to Rockcliffe than to Colvend. The architect was Peter Macgregor Chalmers, well-known in his day as a specialist church designer with a fondness for the pre-Gothic Romanesque style.

Corsock

James Clerk Maxwell

South of the village is **Glenlair**, the home of the most influential scientific thinker of the nineteenth century, James Clerk Maxwell. The original house was built around 1820 by his landowning father John; James enlarged and improved it in 1867.

Of **James Clerk Maxwell** (1831-79) Albert Einstein said 'One scientific epoch ended and another began with James Clerk Maxwell'. Clerk Maxwell's writings, across a prodigious range of topics, are virtually impenetrable for the lay reader. The handiest summary of his achievements is to be found on a commemorative plaque outside the kirk at nearby Parton where he is buried:

> His short life was rich in distinguished contributions to every branch of physical science – heat, light, mechanics. Above all by unifying the theories of electricity and magnetism he established a sure foundation for modern physics, electrical engineering and astronomy, and prepared the way for radio communication and television.

Clerk Maxwell was actually born in Edinburgh. His family moved to Glenlair when he was an infant and, though his professional life took him far afield, he returned to Glenlair as often as possible for the rest of his life. His Stewartry rural upbringing turned him into a skilled horseman, but his sensitivity to suffering caused him to dislike hunting and fishing.

He apparently also became accomplished at Scottish country dancing. Who knows what ground-breaking theory, destined to change our view of the world, may have been formulated in his busy brain as his feet processed through a Gay Gordons?

At first he was educated at home. In 1841 he was sent to Edinburgh Academy, where, owing to a certain oddness of character, he was nicknamed Dafty. While still at school, his paper on ovals was read on his behalf to the Royal Society of Edinburgh (he was too young to deliver it himself). He went on to Edinburgh University and, while still a student, produced theories of astounding originality, many of his experiments being conducted during vacations at Glenlair. In 1850 he became a postgraduate student at Cambridge and was elected a Fellow of Trinity College in 1855.

His sick father was keen that his son should spend more time at Glenlair. To make this more feasible, Clerk Maxwell accepted a professorship in natural philosophy [what a Scot calls physics] at Marischal College in Aberdeen, though his father, to whom he was close, died before he took up the post. While in Aberdeen he married the daughter of the college principal. Both committed Christians, they were exceptionally devoted to each other. The marriage, however, was childless.

In 1860 he moved to a similar post at King's College, London. He resigned in 1865, and retreated to Glenlair, continuing to experiment and write. In 1871 he was lured southwards again with an offer of the first professorship of experimental physics at Cambridge and the opportunity to run the new Cavendish Laboratory.

Clerk Maxwell was notorious for the difficulty people had in understanding what he was trying to say. He was said to have had such a quick mind that it ran ahead of his tongue. Anyone who has tried reading his *A Dynamical Theory of the Electro Magnetic Field* will appreciate the problem, though the same book has been described by Professor R V Jones as 'one of the greatest leaps ever achieved in human thought'.

As is often the case with the cerebrally gifted, there was another side to him, a boyish frivolity which found expression in light verse, as in this extract from *Valentine by a Telegraph Clerk to a Telegraph Clerk:*

The tendrils of my soul are twined
With thine, though many a mile apart,
And thine in close-coiled circuits wind
Around the needle of my heart.

O tell me, when along the line
From my full heart the message flows
What currents are induced in thine?
One click from thee will end my woes.

or his much-anthologised parody, *Rigid Body Sings*:

Gin a body meet a body
Flyin' through the air,
Gin a body hit a body,
Will it fly? and where?
Ilka impact has its measure,
Ne'er a' ane hae I,
Yet a' the lads they measure me,
Or, at least, they try.

Gin a body meet a body
Altogether free,
How they travel afterwards
We do not always see.
Ilka problem has its method
By analytics high;
For me, I ken na ane o' them,
But what the waur am I?

His jocularity extended to the way he would sometimes address letters to his father: John Clerk Maxwell Esq., Posty Knowswhere, Kirkpatrick Durham, Dalbeattie.

Clerk Maxwell was still in Cambridge when he died of stomach cancer at the age of 48 (the same age at which his mother died, from the same cause). Although by then Glenlair had been transferred to Corsock parish and he had been an elder there, he was buried in Parton kirkyard beside his parents (see Parton).

Corsock

Glenlair

Most of Glenlair was gutted by fire in 1929. The estate was purchased by the Ferguson family in 1950 and in 1993 the surviving servants' wing was converted into a dwelling.The Maxwell At Glenlair Trust was set up to restore the main house which had been steadily deteriorating since the 1929 fire.

The rest of Corsock is dominated by associations with **Alexander Murray Dunlop**, a central figure in the Disruption of 1843, when about one third of the Church of Scotland ministers broke away in an argument over the extent of state patronage. The secessionists, who rejected state interference, formed their own Free Church of Scotland. As well as MP for Greenock, Dunlop was a lawyer and acted as legal adviser to the ministers of the Disruption. He is depicted in David Octavius Hill's famous multiple portrait of the Free Church signatories.

Dunlop lived at **Corsock House**. This was built around 1800, but in 1853 Dunlop had it extended in Scots Baronial style by the then fashionable architect David Bryce.

The present Corsock **kirk** was originally built for the Free Church, presumably under Dunlop's influence, during 1851-2. Inside the kirk he gets a memorial bust (he died in 1870), while the granite obelisk on the hill opposite is his too. The original kirk in Corsock is now converted into a house called **Kirk Lynn**. James Clerk Maxwell's father was instrumental in its being built in 1838. A Clerk Maxwell memorial window was transferred from it to the present parish kirk. The window incorporates the words he is said to have quoted repeatedly shortly before he died: 'Every good and perfect gift is from above'.

Kirk Lynn

Creetown

You can arrive in Creetown and see not a soul and, if the weather is dreich and there's no sunshine to make the characteristic granite buildings sparkle, this can seem like a village suddenly deserted by its inhabitants. Or is it early-closing *every* day in these parts?

But hold on! This is a place of pilgrimage for the pagan followers of the sexy cult movie *The Wicker Man*; this is where fans of country and western music converge every September for the annual festival; this is where, of an evening, you may hear the happy sound of the famous Creetown Silver Band. Clearly, there is more to Creetown than meets the eye on a wet day in winter.

Creetown's original importance was as the place where pilgrims heading for the shrine of St Ninian at Whithorn got the **ferry** across the Cree to Wigtown. In those days the village was known as Ferrytown of Cree. In the eighteenth century its development became more planned under the direction of local 'improving' landowner John McCulloch of Barholm, whose mansion (now demolished) was designed by the Adam brothers. McCulloch was instrumental in Creetown being created a burgh of barony in 1792. The laird attempted to industrialise the economy, but the lead-shot mill, the cotton mill and the tannery did not last.

The local **granite** was already well-known when in the early 1830s the Liverpool Dock Trustees took out leases on the Glebe and Kirkmabreck quarries. They had been looking for deposits with easier access to the coast for transportation by sea. The granite is in perpendicular stata, and whole blocks could be wedged out without blasting. Schooners transported the material from the nearby quay: between 1831 and 1848 annual voyages between Creetown and Liverpool varied from 40 to 289.

Disused quarry, Creetown

Creetown

Quarry workers

   Employment fluctuated: in 1834 there were 450 workers; ten years later the number was down to 160. When demand was low, many of the quarrymen and their families emigrated. By 1903 Liverpool had no further use for Creetown granite.

   The Glebe quarry continued to be worked intermittently until the end of the twentieth century. Most of the documents relating to its history were lost in a house fire.

For the quarry workers there was recreational relief from their labours in the making of music. The **Creetown Silver Band** was formed in 1880 when £20 was raised to buy twenty instruments. The twenty founding members knew nothing about music, but, after two years of practice, they were able to make their first public appearance. Within a couple of decades, Creetown were the Galloway champions. Though the band's fortunes have been affected over the years by trade depressions, world wars and enforced emigration, it continues to blow hard. In 1997 a new hall was officially opened, the guest of honour being John Gracie, a Creetown player who went on to become Principal Trumpet with the Scottish National Orchestra.

Creetown
Silver Band

By 2006 a makeover of Creetown's **Adamson Square** was completed. The design is a homage to the granite tradition. But that tradition is now so much a thing of the past that the granite required for construction of the new-look square was imported from China! The supplier explained:

> Creetown's granite is just no longer available. We've had the last few rainy-day blocks out of there. Now we source most of our stone from Portugal or China. Given the option between local and imported stone, we'd opt for local if we could. Creetown's one of the better placed quarries in Britain for shipment by sea – it's easy for boats to get in and out. When laid, Chinese granite is almost identical to Creetown granite – it's the closest you can get.

The refurbished square is packed with meaning: the wavy steps represent the seashore, while the strange-looking poles by the bandstand symbolise the salmon stake-nets of the Cree. The sculpture is by **Hideo Furuta** (1949-2007), a Japanese artist who came to live and work in Creetown in the 1990s. Born in Hiroshima, he trained as an artist in Tokyo. He was so determined to master the medium of granite that in the early 1980s he deserted his academic life and went to work as a carver with the quarrymen of Kurahashi Island.

Striking buildings made of authentic Creetown granite abound. The village's best-known landmark, the **Clock Tower**, was erected in 1897 to mark Queen Victoria's Diamond Jubilee. Sitting high up at the end of Kirk Brae, **Kirkmabreck parish kirk** (1831-4) is, however, not of granite but of the Stewartry's other main native building material, whinstone.

The building now most likely to attract the curious is the **Ellangowan Hotel**, built in 1898. It takes its name from a location (frequently associated with nearby Barholm Castle) in Sir Walter Scott's novel, *Guy Mannering*. But fiction of a very different kind is

Old and new granite: Adamson Square with the Clock Tower and Hideo Furuta's sculpture

the pull nowadays. The hotel's bar provided the interior scenes for the 'Green Man' pub in the 1970s movie *The Wicker Man* (the exterior shots were of another establishment, in Gatehouse of Fleet). The weirdness of the film is matched by the strangeness of its cultish fans, for whom the Ellangowan is an unmissable stop on the location trail (see Part 2 - The Movie).

Rocks of a more colourful kind now bring visitors to Creetown: the collection of minerals, crystals and gemstones on display at the **Creetown Gem Rock Museum**, housed in a former school of 1857 (the replacement school of 1965 has been described as being 'in the Festival of Britain manner'). The museum was started in 1971, and ten years later the Stephenson family, long-time visitors to the area, took over.

Unlikely as it may seem, Creetown has a connection with pioneering feminism. Cassencarie House, south of the village, was home for some fifty years to **Mona Caird** (1854-1932), author of *The Morality of Marriage and other Essays on the Status and Destiny of Women* (1897).

Born on the Isle of Wight, she married the laird of Cassencarie, James Caird (died 1921). She argued for equality in marriage so as to 'bring us to the end of the patriarchal system'. She put her ideas into a series of novels published between 1883 and 1915. In *The Daughters of Danaus* (1894), Algitha decides to defy her family in Scotland by leaving for London in search of freedom from inevitably becoming the property of a husband:

> ...I want to spread my wings. And why should I not? Nobody turns pale when Ernest [her brother] wants to spread *his*. How do I know what life is like, or how best to use it, if I remain satisfied with my present ignorance? How can I even appreciate what I possess, if I have nothing to compare it with? Of course, the truly nice and womanly thing to do is to remain at home, waiting to be married. I have elected to be *un*womanly.

Mona Caird has been described by an expert in Victorian fiction as 'one of the most aggressive of the New Woman novelists'. She also wrote passionately in favour of the temperance movement and against animal experimentation. In the fashion of upper-class literary types, she also had a home at Hampstead in London. But, when she died, Cassencarie House was still in her ownership. A hotch-potch of sixteenth-century tower-house and eighteenth-century mansion-house plus nineteenth-century Baronial titivations, it is now largely ruinous. It may never have survived Mrs Caird's fulminations against the established order!

Harbour Street is a reminder of Creetown's maritime past. Its relationship with the sea changed when the A75 by-pass was built across the opening into Wigtown Bay. The coming of the by-pass, however, was warmly greeted by a local bard:

> Man, isn't it jist great:
> Nae mair windaes that vibrate,
> Nae juggernauts wi heavy load
> Scootin' up the nerra road,
> Nae hissin', screechin' brakes,
> Nae doors that bang, rattle and shake.
> Ferry Toon, ye look real braw;
> A bonnier picture ye couldna draw.

To a large extent twenty-first-century Creetown thrives on its memories. The enterprising **Creetown Heritage Museum**, set up in a former garage in the 1990s, ensures that there's no forgetting, not even of painful memories like the devastating floods of 1954.

One thing *is* being forgotten, however – that Creetown is traditionally part of the Stewartry of Kirkcudbright. The local government reorganisation of the 1970s unfortunately moved the village into the administrative district of Wigtown and its official postal town is now Newton Stewart across the Cree in Wigtownshire. But Creetonians with a strong sense of history insist that they still belong to Kirkcudbrightshire (see Introduction).

The current ambiguity around Creetown's identity erupted into a public row in the summer of 2007. *The Galloway Gazette* ran a front-page splash under the headline 'Creetown in Wigtownshire?' The story was about the official opening ceremony for the refurbished Adamson Square. The dignitary invited to officiate was the Lord Lieutenant of Wigtownshire. Some of the village's Stewartry loyalists boycotted the event in protest. In an astounding display of ignorance the organisers, the Dumfries and Galloway Arts Association, defended the invitation by claiming that 'Creetown was once in Wigtownshire.' A Stewartry spokesperson stated the correct position: 'The Lord Lieutenant of the Stewartry covers up to the River Cree in the west, historically the boundary of the Stewartry and Wigtownshire.'

One affinity with its neighbouring county is beyond doubt, though. Travellers going from east to west may notice that the Irish-tinged speech of the Shire begins around here.

Crocketford

Also known as Ninemile Bar (in the days of the turnpike trusts there was a toll-bar here nine miles west of Dumfries), this village on the A75 had the strangest of origins. It was first developed by a sect of fanatics known as the **Buchanites**. They were followers of a crazed harridan by the name of Elspeth Buchan - or 'Lucky Buchan' - who was born in Banffshire in 1738.

She recruited her first band of followers at Irvine in Ayrshire, including a kirk minister, a Mr White, who fell under her spell and deserted his wife and two young children. She convinced them all that she had divine connections. They addressed her as 'Friend Mother in the Lord'. She brainwashed them into believing that they could bypass death and ascend straight to Heaven. To this end they built high platforms in the expectation that the angels would come down and whisk them off to everlasting happiness. Unfortunately, on one occasion the platform was toppled by a gust of wind and Mrs Buchan landed with a thud. This failure sorely tested the faith of some, who emigrated.

In the early 1780s they moved to a farm near Thornhill in Dumfriesshire before settling in the Stewartry, first at the farm of Auchengibbert and later in what is now Crocketford.

When Mrs Buchan died in 1791 her expected heaven-wards journey did not apparently take place. But, to her adherents, it was ever imminent, and, so as not to impede her resurrection, her coffin was kept above ground. When her last disciple died in 1841, his coffin was laid on top of hers so that, if she ever rose, he would be lifted up with her.

At the height of its fervour, the movement numbered some sixty suckers. Pending resurrection, they busied themselves building and making. They were innovative spinners of yarn; their products had quite a reputation.   A rump of the sect was still in existence, but diminishing rapidly, when John Mactaggart wrote about the Buchanites in his *Scottish Gallovidian Encyclopedia*:

> She would allow none of her followers to marry, or have any love-dealings with other; so the tribe soon weeded away and became thin. It is said there were many *bastard bairnies* appeared amongst them; but that they hardly ever let them behold the light.

A once-popular Victorian writer of light verse, **Alexander Anderson** (1845-1909), was brought up in Crocketford. He usually wrote under the pen-name of 'Surfaceman', a reference to his early working years with the Glasgow and South-Western Railway Company. His *Songs of the Rail* came out in 1878. He was born in Dumfriesshire but, when he was three, his family moved to Crocketford, where he attended the village school. It was while he was a railwayman that he started to educate himself in foreign languages and literature. He left the railway and took up librarianship in Edinburgh. He is best remembered for his Scots lullabies. In the most famous, *Cuddle Doon*, a mother is having her usual difficulty in settling the children at bedtime until...

> At length they hear their faither's fit,
> An', as he steeks the door,
> They turn their faces to the wa',
> While Tam pretends to snore.
> 'Hae a' the weans been gude?' he asks,
> As he pits aff his shoon.
> 'The bairnies, John, are in their beds,
> An' lang since cuddled doon.'

In prehistoric times nearby **Milton Loch** was the site of a crannog, an awesomely clever dwelling constructed upon wooden piles driven (without machinery) into the water bed. A crannog here was excavated in 1953 when, owing to a prolonged spell of dry weather, the level of the loch was exceptionally low. It may have been built originally in the fourth century BC, continuing in use possibly until the second century AD.

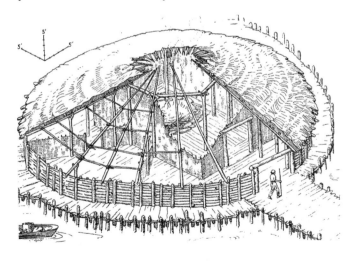

A crannog of the type found in Milton Loch

47

Crossmichael

Crossmichael can surprise you. It may look like a one-street clachan but that is before you have noticed road names like Old Ferry Road and Riverside Lane. What seems to be just another landlocked village spread along a main road takes on a wholly unexpected aspect when viewed from the west. This reveals a busy marina on the River Dee/Loch Ken; and, at certain times of the year, 'Crossmichael-Sur-Mer' might seem a more appropriate name.

The *cross*, dedicated to *St Michael*, is no longer in place. But the village pump is still there, re-instated in 1994. There has been less luck, though, for the village Gala Committee, after whose AGM in 2004 the following announcement was placed on the community notice-board:

> Several members offered their resignations from the committee and no-one was willing or able to fill these or other offices. It was therefore proposed and agreed that the Committee shall be suspended due to lack of support.

At the northern end of the village, in an elevated position, is the handsome white-washed **kirk**. This is substantially of the mid-eighteenth century, but its very unusual round steeple attached to the frontage is from the previous century.

As with many Stewartry kirkyards, graves of Covenanters abound. But the most eye-catching burial monument is that of Sir William Gordon of Greenlaw (a 1740s mansion due south of Crossmichael). The central tablet was re-faced in 1996, with 'wording reproduced from the original to the extent it remained decipherable'. The omissions intrigue:

Crossmichael Kirk

> This monument is erected
> by his disconsolate Widow
> In Memory Of the bed of

The bed of what? We shall never know. And: 'Religion has lost a...' We can only guess.

My Father's House (1969) is an account by Pauline Neville of her life as a daughter of the manse in Crossmichael during the 1920s and '30s. Her father, the Rev J A Fisher, became convenor of the Stewartry of Kirkcudbright County Council. During the Second World War he was enthusiastic about his Home Guard duties, and on Sundays he would wear his military uniform underneath the clerical garb:

> Somehow, his short bulky figure looked ungainly in battledress, and the large head only seemed to increase the incongruity of the performance.
> Each time that I heard the great, booted feet come up the steps from the vestry into the pulpit, I received a shock. The parishioners had got used to it, and knew that as soon as Church was over, father would be off on some exercise. But I found the heavy feet strangely unsymbolic of his delicate approach to everything else in life.

Another Crossmichael memoir, ***Letter of a Lifetime*** (1999), is a touching account of Franz Münchow's journey from Polish prisoner-of-war to Stewartry farmer. He was sent to work for the Gourlays on their two farms, Mountaintop and Craigenally, which lie to the north-east of the village. On his first day he was greeted by the

49

aroma of coffee and freshly baked scones, and he immediately felt at home. Soon he moved from the POW camp to become the Gourlays' full-time employee and lodger, and when he gained his freedom he decided to stay on. He had fallen in love with the Gourlays' daughter Jessie. But the declaration was slow to come. He was shy and felt unworthy because he did not have 'my own home with an oven'. Finally the subject is broached:

> Miss Jessie reassured me, 'Dear Franz, we have our own home with a stove, thanks to you and your endless work here. Since your first day, we have worked together.'
> ...I held out my arms and without saying a word, she came into my arms and laid her head on my chest. There I was, for the first time in my life, with a woman, not from my family, held in my arms. An incredible experience.

Franz stayed for the rest of his life in the Crossmichael area. He wrote his life-story in Polish at the request of his daughter Jane. The two of them translated it into English. It had originally been meant as a family heirloom for future generations, but now the world at large can read his gentle tale.

Culgruff House, overlooking the village from the east, was built in 1889, a free-style mix of Scots Baronial and English Jacobean. It is said to have been a wedding-present from its original owner to his bride. For a time in the twentieth century it was a hotel.

Culgruff House

Dalbeattie

It is known as 'the granite town', but Dalbeattie's first phase of prosperity pre-dates the large-scale working of its nearby granite deposits. The waterway known as the Dalbeattie Burn is the key to its concerted development from the 1780s by two local landowners. The downhill movement of the burn provided power for a series of mills processing corn and paper. Where the burn enters the River Urr at Dub o' Hass was the town's **harbour**. Today the effects of silting may make it seem unlikely that Dalbeattie was once a thriving port but throughout the nineteenth century schooners brought goods in and out, and passenger steamships operated between here and Liverpool and Whitehaven.

Schooners at Dub o' Hass

Though **granite** had already been used on a small scale for the making of millstones, it was not until the 1820s that the Craignair quarry began to be exploited in a big way. The first major customer was the Liverpool Docks Board. Dalbeattie granite was also used in the building of the Bank of England and the Thames Embankment in London, the Eddystone lighthouse in the English Channel and the harbour at Valletta on Malta.

At its busiest, some four hundred men were engaged in the quarry. After the railway arrived in the middle of the nineteenth century, the station and the Craignair quarry were linked by an overhead ropeway with buckets to carry the granite. The squeak of its mechanism was a familiar sound in the town until the 1950s.

Dalbeattie

The Round House and Dalbeattie Town Hall

Today the granite industry is not what it was. In recent years it has been restricted to providing just gravel for road works. But it has left its distinctive mark on the town's architecture, notable buildings including the **Town Hall** of 1861-2 and the eye-catching Victorian cornerpiece known as **The Round House**.

The granite tradition has now been taken under the wing of the heritage industry. In 2003 the town held its first Festival of Granite, a gathering more of artists than of artisans. According to a newspaper report at the time, the Stewartry-based Japanese sculptor Hideo Furuta 'ran workshops in conjunction with Scottish Ballet for local schoolchildren, introducing them to movement and mime using a number of granite spheres he had created'. The old quarrymen may have turned in their graves (topped with granite stones, of course).

Dalbeattie's most revered local hero is **William McMaster Murdoch**, First Officer on the RMS Titanic in 1912 when it hit an iceberg in the Atlantic and sank with the loss of some 1500 lives.

William McMaster Murdoch

The Murdoch memorial on Dalbeattie Town Hall wall

When the James Cameron movie, *Titanic*, was released in 1997, Dalbeattie folk were horrified to discover that Murdoch had been inaccurately portrayed as a bribe-taking villain who shot himself in shame. Twentieth Century Fox had to apologise to the town, and donated £5000 to the fund for the Murdoch Memorial Prize which local pupils still compete for annually.

Edingham at the northern boundary of Dalbeattie has two historic sites, four centuries apart in origin. The ruins of Edingham Castle date from the early 1500s, while nearby are the eerily preserved remains of a World War II explosives factory which in its heyday employed a workforce of 2,600.

Buittle Old Tower - the latest in a long line of fortified dwellings on this site

To the west of the town, **Buittle** (pronounced *bittle*), on the far bank of the River Urr, is where the twelfth- and thirteenth-century Lords of Galloway had a motte-and-bailey castle. Dervorguilla (died 1289 or 1290), daughter of the last of these hereditary rulers, spent much of her widowhood here, supervising two great memorials to her late husband John de Balliol: the building of Sweetheart Abbey, in New Abbey, and the founding of Balliol College in Oxford. She did not live to see her hapless son, also John, crowned (but only thanks to English intervention) King of Scotland, nor to see him subsequently reviled as 'Toom Tabard' [empty coat]. In 1991 the Stewartry Archaeological Trust began a series of excavations here. The only building now intact, Buittle Old Tower, came some three centuries later.

To the south-west, on the road to Castle Douglas, the ruined **Buittle Old Kirk** (adjacent to the present parish kirk, built 1817-19) is substantially medieval and may have been financed by Dervorguilla.

St John's Town of
Dalry

L et's first of all make sense of the **name**. St John the Baptist
was venerated by the medieval military-monastic order known
as the Knights Templar. The Templars were founded at the time
of the Crusades to the Holy Land: their knights provided protection for Christian pilgrims against Muslim attacks. They grew into
a powerful and hugely wealthy international organisation, owning
land and property throughout Europe – including, it would seem,
the parish of Dalry.

The village ('town' seems a bit of an overstatement) was originally known as St John's Clachan [hamlet]. For everyday purposes, it is just plain Dalry, and is sometimes sentimentalised as
The Clachan. But care must be taken to distinguish it from Dalry
in Ayrshire, about which the Rev C H Dick wrote in his 1916 *Highway and Byways in Galloway and Carrick*: 'I have nothing to say
against that place with its coal-pits, blast furnaces, and cotton and
woollen factories; but I wish to guard against any reader going
thither and then announcing that this book is full of misleading
information'.

To complicate matters further, the town used to be referred to
as Old Galloway, to differentiate it from nearby New Galloway
with which in the past it has had a sniffy relationship.

St John's Chair

Dalry is immensely proud of an old
seat-shaped stone known as **St
John's Chair**. There may well remain some pious folk hereabouts
who still believe that the great Baptist himself placed his behind on it.

The oldest visible evidence of
Dalry's antiquity is the twelfth-
century **motte** just to the north of the
kirk. Nothing remains of the castle
that would have surmounted it. The
regularity of the motte's shape suggests it was artificial.

The present **parish kirk**, prettily positioned at the end of an ave-
nue of lime-trees, is - by comparison - recent (built 1830-32). The
adjacent crow-stepped construction known as the Gordon Aisle

Dalry Kirk

was built in 1546 for the Gordons of Lochinvar and was originally part of an earlier kirk.

From its earliest times, hospitality has been one of Dalry's staple trades. It was a popular watering-hole along the medieval **pilgrims' route**, the Edinburgh-Whithorn circuit for Christians heading westward to pay homage to St Ninian or, as in the case of King James IV in the 1490s, to seek forgiveness for sins committed.

The modern-day pilgrims seeking a bed for the night are worshippers of wholesome living, walkers along the **Southern Upland Way**. This long-distance, coast-to-coast path connects with Dalry via a suspension bridge across the Water of Ken at the point where the earlier pilgrims took the ferry.

Dalry acquired its present layout towards the end of the eighteenth century as a 'planned village' under the patronage of the Earl of Galloway. Its core housing and principal buildings date from the nineteenth century. The **Town Hall** was built in 1859 and remodelled between 1895 and 1897.

In Dalry there is no getting away from the bloody history of the seventeenth-century **Covenanters**, the fanatical defenders of Scottish Presbyterianism against the British Crown's clumsy and cruel attempts to impose Anglican forms of worship.

It was in Dalry that the Pentland Rising of 1666 had its origin. A skirmish with government troops in the village escalated into a massive protest march on Edinburgh, but the Covenanter force of about 900 was routed in the Pentland Hills south of the capital by around 3000 soldiers. Hundreds were killed, either on the battlefield or during the subsequent flight. More were captured and sen-

Dalry

tenced to death. Like all Stewartry kirkyards, Dalry's is well-stocked with Covenanter gravestones.

As if these reminders were not sufficient, in 2004 the Scottish Covenanter Memorials Association presented a commemorative sculpture to Dalry. It is made of three tons of stainless steel, and the design takes its theme from the 'Burning Bush' in Exodus chapter 3. It has been placed next to a children's playground – now, let that be a warning!

Covenanter sculpture

Earlstoun is a name that resonates in the vicinity of Dalry. Part of the sixteenth/seventeenth-century Earlstoun Castle still stands. The castle is associated with the Gordons who took a prominent part in the anti-episcopalian movement. Earlstoun Loch now serves as a reservoir for Earlstoun power station, part of the gigantic Galloway hydro-electric scheme (see Part 2 - The Hydro).

North-east of Dalry, **Knocknalling** is where one of the big names of the Manchester cotton trade was brought up. John Kennedy (1769-1865) went to Lancashire to serve his apprenticeship as a joiner. He was good at inventing machines, and through this he became a wealthy magnate, a friend of James Watt of steam-engine fame and of George Stephenson of locomotive fame. Kennedy was one of the first directors of the Liverpool and Manchester Railway.

With his wealth he bought up land all around his birthplace, including Knocknalling estate, and in the 1840s built a 'Tudor'-style mansion. He even planned setting up a cotton-mill here and had a mill-race cut through rock, but nothing came of it.

Kennedy returned to his birthplace a great deal until old age made the journey too difficult. In his published writings Kennedy showed himself to be a plutocrat with progressive ideas. On the Poor Laws, he wrote: '...the poor have a right to be supported from the surplus capital of their employers which they have helped to produce'.

Dundrennan

The glories of Gothic architecture, the tragedy of Mary Queen of Scots, training for World War Two, a rock-music festival... all feature in the story of this tiny place where today you could imagine nothing ever happening.

Cistercian monks from Yorkshire settled here, by invitation of Fergus, Lord of Galloway, in 1141 and embarked on an **abbey** building programme that continued for the best part of a century. First came the presbytery and transepts at the east end, followed by the nave, and finally, to the south, the cloister, chapter-house and various domestic buildings.

The Cistercians were an austere order dedicated to finding tranquillity well away from secular society. When they surveyed this secluded hollow in the hills, they must have felt that they had found a site answering exactly to their needs.

The abbey did not, however, survive the Reformation of 1560. It was already in a state of disrepair by then, and before long it was abandoned by the monks. Local builders helped themselves to the stone blocks. However, the east end remained in use as a parish church until 1742.

In 1839, when the circuit judge Lord Cockburn visited the ruins, he was appalled by the lack of care for an ancient monument:

Ruins of Dundrennan Abbey

> ...every other feeling is superseded by one's horror and indignation at the state in which it is kept...Not a trace of it will be discoverable in fifty years...It is a humiliating, national scandal.

He blamed the landowners, the Maitlands, with whom, ironically, he was staying at the time: 'My excellent and esteemed host...is the chief delinquent'. Five years later, back again with the Maitlands, he triumphantly reported in his journal:

> The objurgation which I have recorded in 1839 was freely administered verbally. This roused Thomas Maitland, now of Dundrennan, and he roused Lord Selkirk and others; and the result is that the Commissioners of Woods and Forests have cleaned out the rubbish, and drained the ground, and made some judicious repairs, and cleared away the abominable offices of the manse, and enclosed the whole. It is still far from what a reverenced ruin ought to be, because its preservation requires much more pinning and cementing, and purity; but compared to what it was, it is humanity to barbarism.

Mary Queen of Scots

Before the last monks departed, they had the excitement of entertaining a celebrity of the sixteenth century. This is where in 1568 the fugitive **Mary Queen of Scots** spent what turned out to be her last-ever night in Scotland. She was on the run after defeat at the Battle of Langside. Her aide Lord Herries escorted her to the south-west where she still had a strong following. With her distinctive red-gold hair shaved off to avoid recognition, she was guided, according to the traditional account, along the remote passes of the Glenkens and down the west bank of the River Ken towards Tongland. North of Ringford, Queenshill is reputed to be where she stopped for a rest. Later she described to her uncle in France the privations and humiliation of this arduous journey on horseback:

> I have endured injuries, calumnies, imprisonment, famine, cold, heat, flight not knowing whither, 92 miles across the country without stopping or alighting, and then I have had

to sleep upon the ground and drink sour milk, and eat oat-meal without bread, and have been three nights like the owls...

Mary and her party were heading for the Maxwell stronghold at Terregles in the east. It is thought that on the way she may have spent a night at Corra Castle near Kirkgunzeon. At Terregles, despite passionate advice to the contrary, the queen took the disastrous decision to throw herself upon the mercy of her cousin Queen Elizabeth of England. She made her way to Dundrennan. On the afternoon of Sunday May 16, 1568, she and her attendants piled into a fishing-boat (the spot from which she is reputed to have embarked is still called Port Mary) and landed at Workington on the Cumberland coast. She never saw Scotland again.

The parish is known as **Rerrick**. A fragment of the original Rerrick Kirk is in the cemetery to the south-east of the village. The present parish kirk took over in 1865. A 1780s building that once housed the school remains, along with its mid-nineteenth century replacement. The village school, however, closed in 2004.

South of the village, by the shore, there are still visible remains of a once thriving community called **Abbey Burnfoot** or Netherlaw Burnfoot. In the second half of the nineteenth century, there were a dozen or so salmon fishermen's cottages, one or two larger houses, a harbour, a grocer and a coal merchant.

This green and sheltered spot is far removed from any of the twentieth-century theatres of war – yet in two ways the Second World War impacted upon the area.

Abbey Burnfoot, Dundrennan, as it was

Dundrennan

In 1942 the **Ministry of Defence** took possession of 4,700 acres of farmland along the coast between Dundrennan and Kirkcudbright. The original purpose was for training troops for a Continental invasion. Over the years the base's function has alternated between military training and weapons testing. Since 1942 virtually all of it has been inaccessible to the public; popular bays were taken away from the people who had enjoyed them. It remains an adventure-playground for grown-up boys with lethal toys.

The other connection with modern warfare: in July 1944, in the village itself, an **American warplane** crashed accidentally into a house. Of the five family members, only one survived; the two crewmen also died. The site of the destroyed house was never built upon again.

To the north-east, at East Kirkcarswell farm, the annual **Wickerman Festival** is held. The first was in 2002. It is a kind of mini-Glastonbury (but weirder). The festival takes its name from the film *The Wicker Man* (see Part 2 - The Movie).

A shaped hedge marks the site of the Wickerman Festival

Gatehouse of Fleet

It is difficult to believe that this douce little town, so favoured by genteel retirees (overwhelmingly from England), was once dubbed **'The Glasgow of the South'**. In the late-eighteenth and early-nineteenth centuries it was throbbing with industrial enterprises. The remaining fabric of those times (now largely gentrified into smart dwellings) led the historian John Butt to give this assessment of modern Gatehouse of Fleet: 'a rare and beautiful example of an arrested industrial village and a source of satisfaction for the industrial archaeologist'.

Its post-industrial tranquillity is well captured by the title of an Edwardian guide to the town: *A Nook in Galloway*. And it has been even more of a nook since a by-pass diverted the A75 traffic from its High Street.

Cally House, the great granite-faced mansion that peeps above the woodland of the Cally Estate, is the clue to Gatehouse's dash for growth in the eighteenth century. Now a hotel, the 'Cally Palace' was built in the 1760s for the landowner **James Murray**. It was he who planned the transformation of an area consisting of a solitary 'Gait House' [gait=road] into a boom town of mills, tanneries, soap-works, brickworks and breweries.

Murray's mansion
- now the Cally Palace Hotel

The Mill on the Fleet

The Water of Fleet was too low to provide the required power, so a supply was piped downhill from Loch Whinyeon four miles away and fed along both sides of the town through a system of lades. Murray went into partnership with a Yorkshire entrepreneur called Birtwhistle whose workers were housed in the street that now takes their employer's name.

By 1793 Gatehouse had 160 houses and a population of 1,150. In 1795 the town was created a Burgh of Barony. The Stewartry chronicler Robert Heron noted that Murray of Cally:

> ...had the pleasure of seeing a fine village rise near his principal seat; more orderly in arrangement, more uniformly handsome in its building, happier in its situation than perhaps any other village in Galloway.

However, the same Heron was alarmed by some of the social effects of industrialisation:

> I wish I could honestly add that the morals of these good people have been improved with their circumstances. But prostitution and breaches of chastity have lately become frequent here. Tippling houses are wonderfully numerous. I was informed by the intelligent exciseman of the place that not fewer than an hundred and fifty gallons...of whisky alone...had been consumed here for every week of the last six months...

Despite the rapid rate of development, however, Gatehouse never did become transformed into 'the Glasgow of the South'. It was the regions of Scotland with deposits of coal that triumphed in the later phases of the Industrial Revolution. The building that

Port McAdam: in its heyday and now

since 1991 has been known as **The Mill on the Fleet Visitor Centre** ceased operations as a cotton factory in 1850, though it diversified for a while into manufacturing bobbins – for supply to the coal-belt rivals that had undermined Gatehouse's early progress in the first place.

Bold improvements to the infrastructure of Gatehouse were undertaken by James Murray's son, Alexander. In 1824 he had the meandering River Fleet straightened into a **canal** to enable shipping to reach the town. The channel was dug by tenants from his estate at Donegal in Ireland; their labour here paid off their rent arrears. A quay was subsequently built at **Port McAdam** close to Cardoness Castle.

Alexander Murray also radically changed the eastern approach road into Gatehouse. Originally the route came down into the town along Ann Street, past the 'gait house'. Murray wanted it taken away from the grounds of Cally House. In 1819 he had 'The Cut' blasted through a hillside to the north-east.

For centuries Gatehouse has been a stopping-place on the main route across the South-West to and from the Irish sea-links on the Wigtownshire coast, and so the hospitality trade has always been to the fore. Of its many hostelries, the **Murray Arms Hotel**, established by James Murray in 1760, is the most renowned. It is claimed that during a stay here the poet Robert Burns wrote one of his most famous songs, *Robert Bruce's Address to His Troops at Bannockburn*, more familiarly known by its opening words *Scots Wha Hae*. Since he took the opportunity of a stopover in Gatehouse to get exceedingly drunk, this claim is very dubious (see Part 2 - The Bards).

At the opposite end of the town, the **Anwoth Hotel** (now restored to its earlier name, the Ship) has benefited from its association with the writer Dorothy L Sayers. She was a frequent visitor to the Stewartry, and this is where she lodged before acquiring a holiday-home in Kirkcudbright. The county's artistic community

Gatehouse of Fleet

Barlay Mill

was the backdrop for her Lord Peter Wimsey tale *Five Red Herrings* (1931), and she dedicated the book to the Anwoth's proprietor Joe Dignam, 'kindliest of landlords' (see Part 2 -The Novelists). Although Kirkcudbright became more famous as an artists' colony, Gatehouse can fairly claim to have been ahead in the nurturing of artistic talent. At Barlay Mill to the north of the town, five out of the six children of James and Mary **Faed** achieved fame as painters and etchers, as did three of the next generation. Thomas Faed (1826-1900) was the most conspicuously successful, becoming a member of the Royal Academy in London. John Faed (1819-1902) also flourished in London, but he was the one with the greater longing to be back home. He re-settled in his home town in 1880 (see Part 2 - The Artists).

Until a radical reorganisation of local government in the 1970s, Gatehouse had its own town council. The loss of this local executive power seems to be symbolised in what has happened to the **town hall** on High Street. Completed in 1885, it was re-modelled and partially demolished a century later. The garden at the back is where it once extended to. The other High Street building of civic note is the very distinctive **clock tower**, built in 1871. The people of Gatehouse can rejoice in having a clock tower like no other in the country.

To the south-west, atop a rocky hillock, stands **Cardoness Castle**, the late-fifteenth-century fortified home of the McCullochs. A fighting, argumentative gene ran through generations of the McCullochs. Their tower-house was de-

The Clock Tower

signed to be defensible – but they probably had their feuding neighbours in mind more than the threat of foreign invasion. The castle is equipped with a prison, slits in the stonework for gunfire, and a 'murder-hole', an opening above the entrance from which unwelcome visitors could be robustly dealt with.

Distance was no object to the McCullochs as far as fighting and plundering were concerned. One of them in the early-sixteenth century, known as 'Cutlar' McCulloch, was so familiar as a raider on the Isle of Man that he inspired a Manx proverb:

God keep the good corn, the sheep and the bullock
From Satan, from sin, and from Cutlar McCulloch.

Cardoness Castle

Among earlier visitors to the area were the **Romans**. They built a small fort on the east bank of the Fleet to the north of the present town. Although the Romans surveyed further into the west of Galloway and even contemplated a conquest of Ireland, their presence was never significantly felt in the South-West beyond Gatehouse. Just think of Gatehouse of Fleet as the far western boundary of the great Roman empire!

Gelston

This is where the upwardly mobile founder of Castle Douglas, Sir William Douglas, fulfilled his ultimate fantasy of being a Scots 'laird' with a big 'castle'.

Gelston Castle

Of course **Gelston Castle** is no such thing. It is a Georgian mansion house with retro castellated features, built around 1805. No expense was spared. Its present sorry state of dilapidation makes it difficult to appreciate the scale of ambition that went into this project. The sandstone blocks used were of the very highest quality. The architect may have been Richard Crichton, who designed the Bank of Scotland headquarters on the Mound in Edinburgh. Sir William did not enjoy his new domestic grandeur for long. He died in 1809.

The **Douglas Mausoleum** was built around 1820 in a secluded woodland setting off the road from Gelston to Threave Garden. It is an extraordinary architectural concoction in an ancient Grecian/Egyptian style and is one of the spookier sights of the Stewartry.

The parish here is **Kelton**. The parish kirk is close to the Douglas Mausoleum. It is an undistinguished building of 1805-6. A small fragment of the previous parish kirk is in the kirkyard across the road, a short distance to the south-east.

The Douglas Mausoleum

Girthon

The road leading due south to Sandgreen beach from the A75 brings you to a sign suggesting you are about to enter a place called Girthon. Blink and you could easily miss it. This tiniest of clachans is no more than a few small cottages, the old kirk and the former manse. Girthon, however, has a wider meaning as the name of the parish.

Girthon Kirk

Parts of the now ruined **kirk** date back to late-medieval times but have early-seventeenth-century alterations. It was abandoned around 1818. The adjacent manse, confusingly re-named Girthon Kirk, is substantially of the 1730s, though, according to one architectural historian, its features 'indicate a seventeenth-century house regularised'.

The **kirkyard** has a good collection of eighteenth-century gravestones. One, for a gardener on the Cally estate, has carved representations of a rake, a hoe and a spade. The most significant memorial, however, is for the Covenanting 'martyr', **Robert Lennox**, one of five killed on Kirkconnel Moor in 1685 (see Ringford).

Lennox's stone may be the work of **Robert Paterson**, the fanatically pious mason immortalised as 'Old Mortality' by Sir Walter Scott (see Balmaclellan). According to Scott, Paterson did do work at Girthon. In his introduction to *Old Mortality,* Scott tells a bizarre anecdote. One day Paterson and the kirkyard caretaker were trying to get on with their respective tasks but were increasingly annoyed by a gang of mischievous boys. The youths included the grandsons of a local man who specialised in making wooden domestic utensils. His products had a reputation for giving a reddish tinge to liquids. When one of the boys asked the caretaker what use could be made of the old coffins he had dug up, Paterson interjected: 'Do you not know that he sells them to your grandfather, who makes them into spoons, trenchers, bickers, bowies, and so forth?' Scott continues:

> At this assertion, the youthful group broke up in great confusion and disgust, on reflecting how many meals they had eaten out of dishes which, by Old Mortality's account, were only fit to be used at a banquet of witches or of ghouls.

Word spread around the community, everyone became convinced they now knew where the reddish tinge came from, and the grandfather's business was ruined. If true, the story at least goes to show that 'Old Mortality', for all his solemn obsessiveness, had a hint of a sense of humour.

Girthon was the birthplace of **Dr Thomas Murray** (1792-1872), author of *The Literary History of Galloway* (1822). From the parish school he went to Edinburgh University, where he befriended Thomas Carlyle who became one of the nineteenth century's leading men of letters. He and Carlyle were said to have walked together to Edinburgh at the start of every academic term. Murray trained for the ministry but chose to pursue a career as a writer. Later in life he made a lot of money from a printing business, enabling him to 'crown a youth of labour with an age of ease'. He was a founder, in 1841, of the Edinburgh Galloway Association.

In *The Scottish Gallovidian Encyclopedia,* John Mactaggart dismisses Murray's literary history as a waste of effort:

> …what was the use of rummaging ancient libraries, to know whether a certain priest once lived in a certain parish, and a *priest* who, when all is known of him that can be or *could* be, is worth nothing, he turns out to be a mere common *priest*? Mr. M. is also too in an error, when he thinks that there are, or have been, no literary characters in Galloway but *priests*…

South from the clachan, Rainton Farm is a prodigiously successful example of diversification. The Finlay family have farmed here since 1927. By the 1990s they were looking for a fresh challenge and settled on the idea of making dairy ice-cream. The **Cream o' Galloway** brand was launched in 1994. They also decided to convert the farm to organic; it officially became so in 2001. Their ice-cream and frozen yoghurt products are sold not only by retailers throughout the UK but also direct from the farm as part of a visitor attraction that includes farm walks and an adventure-playground.

Glenlochar

There is much more to Glenlochar and its surroundings than just the 1930s **barrage** that controls the flow of water down to the hydro-electric power station at Tongland (see Part 2 -The Hydro). The present road bridge was built around 1790. But this part of the River Dee has been a crossing-point since ancient times.

Which is why the **Romans** came here and established a base for their various military incursions into the south-west of Scotland. The extent of their settlement here, to the south-east of the present bridge, was not fully understood until the development in the 1940s of archaeological photography from the air. It was then possible to see the outline of what had been a very substantial Roman encampment. Previously it had been thought that the site was that of a vanished abbey. As many as one thousand Roman soldiers at a time may have been accommodated here. The road eastwards from Glenlochar has the classic straightness of a Roman highway.

To the north of Glenlochar is **Balmaghie Kirk** – 'The Kirk above Dee Water'. Of all the Stewartry kirks, this one has, arguably, the bonniest setting, perched on a mound facing Crossmichael on the opposite side of the river.

Although this has been an ecclesiastical site from pre-Reformation times, the present structure dates largely from 1794. A century later, when additions and alterations were made, the then minister, the Rev H M B Reid, wrote a charming account of

Balmaghie
Kirk

Glenlochar

Balmaghie's legendary bee colony that had made its home in the kirk roof-space but had to make way for the improvements:

> …there was a Homeric conflict between the Builder and the Bee. The plaster had been dislodged, and exposed numberless hosts armed for the fray. Three days the battle raged. On the one side it was waged with a smoke-test machine discharging volumes of sulphurous acid; on the other the dauntless bees had only their natural weapon. The issue could not be doubtful. Not a bee was left to tell the tale…Since then desolation reigns in the once busy home of the Kirk Bee. The poor insect has been thoroughly disestablished and disendowed. May the omen be averted!

Balmaghie kirkyard has the usual Stewartry contingent of Covenanters' gravestones. The most conspicuous is that for two 'martyrs', both called David Halliday and buried together:

> One name, one cause, one grave, one heaven do ty
> Their souls to that one God eternally.

Balmaghie's most famous minister was the **Rev John Macmillan**. He was prominent among the diehard Covenanters who would not accept the final settlement in 1690 of the long and damaging Kirk/State quarrel, and who considered the purity of Scottish Presbyterianism to be still tainted by state patronage. Macmillan was appointed to Balmaghie in 1701. It was not long before he fell out with the Kirk authorities, refused to conform, and was fired from his post in 1704. But Macmillan, with the support – sometimes violent – of most of his congregation, refused to budge, and continued to occupy both manse and pulpit for another quarter of a century after being sacked. Meanwhile, his official replacement, the hapless Rev William McKie, had to put up with makeshift accommodation until Macmillan finally left the area in 1727.

The long-suffering McKie had the posthumous satisfaction of an effusive memorial in the kirkyard:

> O Balmaghie! Lament thy loss;
> But boundless grief is vain;
> The much-lov'd Pastor is gone home –
> Death to the Saints is gain.

In the 1850s **scandal** surrounded the brief ministry of another incumbent, William Freeland, an Irishman 'of very genial nature and social habits, indulging, indeed, a freedom of speech not usual among the clergy' (Rev H M B Reid). The General Assembly of the Church of Scotland deposed him in 1853 for what would now be termed 'inappropriate' behaviour towards young ladies of the parish. He fled to the USA, where he was about to secure an appointment with the American Episcopal Church when word of his misdemeanours arrived from Scotland.

The novelist and one-time Free Kirk minister **S R Crockett**, whose childhood home was nearby, had a special affection for Balmaghie:

> All Galloway is divided into three parts – the Stewartry, the Shire, and the parish of Balmaghie. Some have tried to do without the latter division, but their very ill-success has proved their error. The parish of Balmaghie is the *Cor Cordium* [heart of hearts] of Galloway. It is the central parish – the citadel of Gallovidian prejudices.

In later life Crockett regretted that he only ever returned to the kirk for funerals and hoped to make a final return of his own:

> …when the years are over, many or few, and our Galloway requiem, 'Sae he's won awa', is said of me, that is the bell I should like rung. And there in the high corner I should like to lie, if so the fates allot it, among the dear and simple folk I knew and loved in youth. Let them lay me not far from the martyrs, where one can hear the birds crying in the minister's lilac-bushes, and Dee kissing the river grasses, as he lingers a little wistfully about the bonny green kirk-knowe of Balmaghie.

Crockett's wish was granted.

S R Crockett

Crockett's grave
in Balmaghie kirkyard

Glentrool

Glen Trool draws you north-eastwards into the remarkably remote interior of the Stewartry. Here the green lowlands of 'Bonnie Galloway' give way to the 'Grey Galloway' of heather-covered granite peaks and scarily lonesome lochs with exhilarating names: Benyellary ('eagle's hill'), Kirriereoch ('gray corrie'), Curleywee ('windy peak'), Shalloch-on-Minnoch ('hunting-ground in the middle'), Lamachan ('tawny hill') and so on and so forth in a lyrical sequence laid down by our Gaelic-speaking forbears. The main range here is known as The Awful Hand, and its top knuckle is **Merrick**, the highest peak in the south of Scotland.

Of all the fans of these hills, the most intrepid was the Ayrshire journalist James McBain (1849-1941), author of *The Merrick and the Neighbouring Hills* (1929). His final ascent of Merrick was at the age of 83.

In the early 1930s the travel writer H V Morton reached the summit of Merrick and was awestruck by the contrast with what he was used to:

> ...the best view of all was eastward, where the chain of lochs – Loch Enoch, Loch Neldricken and Loch Valley – lie in utter solitude with their wind-swept waters curling over on shores of silver sand. On top of the Merrick you realize the astonishing remoteness of Galloway. Here, far south of Glasgow, is a wilderness deeper than that of the better-known Highlands. Yet a man can breakfast in London and have tea within sight of the Merrick! He can leave Euston at 10 a.m. and be in Newton Stewart shortly after 6 p.m.! It seems impossible that in a few hours anyone could pass from London into such a solitude.

There's a wheen fishy stories about **Loch Enoch** ('icy loch'), the highest stretch of water in Britain. The trout (if they still exist) are said to lack bottom fins. This is put down to the abrasive effect of flapping against the loch's sharp granite sand. The sand used to be collected for the honing of bladed instruments.

The Merrick country is redolent of mystery, fear and paranoia. It is small wonder that this is where the old legend of the **Murder Hole** is set. According to the traditional story, an old woman and her two sons regularly murdered lone travellers and dumped their bodies in the said hole. A young pedlar, taking shelter one stormy night in their cottage, quickly realised their evil intentions and escaped out of his bedroom window. The brothers chased him with a bloodhound. The boy was saved by a fall which caused him to shed blood. The dog, detecting the blood, was so convinced that it had done its job that the boy was able to get away. When he told of his experiences in the nearest village, the inhabitants decided the time had finally come to eradicate this murderous menace. A lynch-mob set out to find the gruesome threesome and hanged them on the spot.

The novelist S R Crockett famously adapted the legend for his bestseller, *The Raiders* (1894). The Ordnance Survey obligingly lends credence to the tale by marking a 'murder hole' on the western fringe of Loch Neldricken. Whether this refers to the traditional tale or to Crockett's re-working of it, is not clear. This is what Crockett's narrator-hero Patrick Heron and his fearless heroine May Maxwell see of the 'hole':

> Now we were on a platform on the north side of Loch Neldricken, but close by the waterside. There was a strange thing beneath us. It was a part of this western end of the loch, level as a green where they play bowls, and in daylight of the same smooth colour; but in the midst a black round eye of water, oily and murky, as though it were without a bottom, and the water a little arched in the middle – a most unwholesome place to look upon.
>
> As she knelt over me May Maxwell pointed it out to me, with the knife which was in her hand.
>
> 'That is their Murder Hole', she said, 'but if we are to lie there we shall not lie there without company.'

Loch Neldricken, James Faed Jnr - showing the 'Murder Hole'

Glentrool

During the First World War there were frantic but groundless rumours that German sea-planes were using the lochs as a base. The suspicions were taken so seriously that military patrols scoured the hills for months on end.

An intriguing by-product of these wartime patrols was the accidental discovery in 1915 of Bronze Age artefacts now known as the **Glen Trool Hoard**. The collection, now in the possession of the National Museums of Scotland, includes an axe, a spear-head and various tools – all made of bronze – plus some amber beads which had probably been part of a necklace. They have been dated at between 1450 and 1200 BC, and, according to their custodians, they were deposited in this hilly region 'almost certainly as a gift to the gods'.

Glen Trool was the scene of a vital armed engagement in Scotland's War of Independence against England. **Bruce's Stone**, overlooking Loch Trool, marks the site of Robert Bruce's against-the-odds victory of 1307 during his tough guerrilla operation against the English army of occupation. Despite being vastly outnumbered, Bruce's men routed their opponents by rolling boulders down the hillside.

Many of the hillsides here, in common with similar land throughout the Stewartry, are now covered by industrial-scale afforestation. **Glentrool village** was built in the early 1950s to house the Forestry Commission employees.

Bruce's Stone, Glen Trool

Haugh of Urr

Haugh (pronounced to rhyme with *loch*) means low-lying land by a river. This crossroads settlement, where the Old Military Road intersects with the valley of the Urr, was once a busy stopping-place with several inns. Up the hill to the north-east is the neighbouring village of Hardgate, now barely separated.

To the south of the village is the twelfth-century **Motte of Urr**, one of the finest examples in Scotland of earthworks for a motte-and-bailey castle, built probably for Walter de Berkeley, the chamberlain to King William I. 'Only perhaps from the air,' writes a recent historian, 'can one appreciate its great size, looking for all the

world like some great earthen battleship stranded on the alluvial river plain.' The site may have been an adaptation of an Iron Age fort.

The foundation-stone of the present **parish kirk**, on the site of earlier churches, was laid in 1914. The kirk was designed by the eminent Glasgow architect Peter MacGregor Chalmers, and completed in 1915. Inside, there is extensive use of marble from Iona. The lectern was paid for by a former maid at the manse, who raised the money by knitting socks. Its most distinguished minister (incumbent from 1806 to 1813) was Alexander Murray, the shepherd's son who became a celebrated linguist and left the parish to become Professor of Oriental Languages at Edinburgh University (see Minnigaff).

Urr Parish Kirk

Local bard **Robert Kerr** (1811-48) is buried in the kirkyard. He specialised in plaintive ditties like *The Widow's Ae Coo*. Through the hostility of her neighbours, the widow ends up with *nae* coo:

> Sae they forced her at length to put Hawkie away,
> An' sair-hearted left her to wear out her day;
> When owre frail to labour, and owre blin' to sew,
> A poor parish pauper they've made o' her noo.

Rather grander incumbents of the cemetery are various generations of the **Herries** family of Spottes Hall, with their own family burial enclosure. Their mansion, on the west side of the village, was built in the 1780s, and added to in the following century.

Kippford

Now a resort for retirees, holiday-homers, amateur mariners and walkers working off a pub lunch at the old Anchor. But, when the sea was less for leisure than for making a living, Kippford was much more of a workaday kind of place, populated by sailors, fisherfolk, quarrymen and shipyard workers. In the pre-railway age the River Urr and Rough Firth were busy trading routes and Kippford was well placed for anchorage and servicing. Only smaller ships could make it as far upstream as Palnackie, while any craft heading for the former harbour at Dalbeattie usually required a horse-powered tow along the narrow, winding upper reaches of the river.

From the early-nineteenth century Kippford was a centre for **shipbuilding**. The last sailing-ship made here was the ill-fated 240-ton *Balcary Lass*, launched in 1884 and lost not long afterwards off Newfoundland. After that the shipyard did only repairs, finally closing down around the outbreak of war in 1914. Writing in the 1920s, a local resident recalled the ship carpenters' twelve-hour shifts and their twice-a-day whisky-breaks:

> It was a pleasure to watch them caulking the sides of a vessel. I think I hear, even yet, the music of their rhythmical blows on the caulking irons as the oakum was being driven into the seams between the planks. But every morning at 11, and every afternoon at 3, the sounds would cease and the men would march away to the Anchor or one of the other public houses for their dram. And just as regularly preparation was made for the reception of these hard sons of toil by the proprietor of the inn who covered every chair-bottom with newspaper to save them from the tar on the clothes of the workmen. The whisky was 2d a

Kippford

Ship under repair with sails drying - Kippford, late-19th century

glass in those days – not the 1s 4d as in post-war times! But even then, this custom added considerably to the repair account of every vessel overhauled.

Granite quarrying was another component of the old Kippford economy. In the early 1900s the Caledonian quarry was employing more than forty men. The stone was brought to the quayside along a tramway.

Kippford was formerly known as **The Scaur** (or Scar), a Scots term for a crag. It was the crags of Kippford that contained those deposits of granite. At one time the crags protruded so far towards the water's edge that the coastal road had to take a diversion onto the beach. Twice a day, therefore, the road was impassable. This tidal inconvenience was removed by the blasting away of the rocky intrusion. 'Kippford' came into more regular usage from the 1870s, 'Kipp' being a long established name in the area (Kipp Brae, Kipp House, the Kipp estate).

The modern name was no doubt considered to be more in keeping with the leisure role that the village took on increasingly from this period. The first boating **regatta** took place in the 1880s, and in 1904 the Urr Yacht Club was founded. Since 1937 the organisation has been known as the Solway Yacht Club. An RNLI inshore **lifeboat** station was opened in 1966. The crew built a new boathouse in 1977 and in 1999 the service switched from a summer-only operation to all-the-year-round.

Kirkandrews

A settlement of some antiquity, with fragments of a medieval kirk and the gravestones of a Covenanting 'martyr' and of the Borgue poet William Nicholson (see Part 2 - The Bards). The St Lawrence Fair, which used to take place every August, was condemned by a local minister as 'a time of great lechery and lewdness and should be suppressed'.

Kirkandrews 'Kirk'

However, the area is now best known for the oddness of its later architecture. Kirkandrews and the mile-and-a-half coastline stretching westwards to Knockbrex on the Carrick shore have the unmistakable imprint of one man's eccentric vision. It is in effect an open-air gallery of architectural follies. Welcome to the mad world of **James Brown** (died 1920), Manchester draper turned Stewartry laird.

Brown – one half of the Manchester department store Affleck and Brown – acquired the Knockbrex estate in 1894 with an eye to retiring to the land of his forbears. Brown must somehow have felt that this lovely stretch of coast was not sufficiently picturesque, for he then embarked on a building programme aimed at overlaying these ancient lands with a fake 'olde-worlde' quaintness.

The folk of the old clachan of Kirkandrews had been content to worship in their tin-clad mission-hall until Brown came along, ripped it down, and built in its place a ridiculous wee pseudo-kirk in the style of a mini-castle, complete with a turret to disguise the chimney. This project was finished in 1906.

Castle Haven Dun

Brown not only built from scratch but also meddled with what was already there, even if it was an historic arte-

79

fact. His principal act of well-meant vandalism took place a short distance due west from Kirkandrews at **Castle Haven Bay**. This is the site of a 'dun', a stone-built homestead possibly of the first century BC and very unusual in this part of Scotland. In 1905 our incorrigible interferer, with more money than sense, set about 'improving' this structure, heightening its walls and thereby causing incalculable confusion for subsequent generations of archaeologists. An eminent Scottish architectural historian commented:

> This extraordinary structure…is as much a monument to the energetic enthusiasm of early 20th century antiquarians as to the needs and aspirations of an iron-age chieftain.

Earlier, around 1900, at the western end of his estate, Brown had built a new family mansion **Knockbrex House** around an earlier building. There was nothing 'olde-worlde' about the domestic amenities, as is obvious from this contemporary account:

> It is now a large and commodious building, with all the latest improvements in heating, lighting, and sanitary arrangements. Large sums have also been expended in improving and beautifying the policies with the introduction of artificial ponds, rockeries, shrubberies, and flower gardens. To Nature lovers, perhaps too much artifice is evident in the landscape gardening scheme.

Given Brown's taste, the style of Knockbrex House seems surprisingly straightforward. But his mania for quaintness was soon let loose again within the grounds, where in 1906 he built a mock-castle – a 'toy fort', as it has been described.

Knockbrex 'Castle'

The house's private beach has its own collection of castellated curiosities, notably a beach-hut in the style of a Moorish castle.

Next for prettification (1911-14) came **Corseyard** farm midway between Knockbrex and Kirkandrews. Here he built a milking parlour in the form of an Italian church and a castellated water-tower/

The 'Coo Palace'

grain-silo. It was not long before the locals dubbed the byre 'the coo-palace', while the water tower, which was meant to serve Knockbrex House, never worked properly – a twofold folly from the start.

Traditional drystane-dykes were apparently not quite good enough for the enclosure of the Brown follies. Walls were built with curious insetting of pebbles collected from the seashore.

North-east of Knockbrex are the remains of **Plunton Castle**, a sixteenth-century stronghold of the Lennox family, whose name continues in the farm called Lennox Plunton, birthplace of the writer John Mactaggart (see Borgue).

Off the Knockbrex shore is **Ardwall Island**, which has a long history of occupation by Christian communities beginning with an Irish settlement possibly as early as the sixth century. Many centuries later, at the height of the smuggling trade, the island was used for the storage of contraband. The smugglers even had the convenience of a tavern. One of its landlords was an Irishman called Larry Higgins, which is why Ardwall Island is often referred to as Larry's Isle. Access to the island is possible only for a short time between tides: misjudging the right time to use the causeway can be fatal, and that is exactly how Larry Higgins met his end.

Ardwall Island (Larry's Isle) from the Carrick shore

Kirkbean

The village's heritage is dominated by pride in its most famous son, John Paul Jones (1747-92), who progressed through privateering to become an American hero. The cottage where he was born is now the **John Paul Jones Museum**. His story is told elsewhere (see Part 2 - The Pirate).

Through his father's employment Jones has a connection with Kirkbean's other outstanding historical figure. **William Craik** (1703-98) developed the estate of Arbigland, where John Paul Jones' father was a gardener. He reputedly also designed its classical mansion, which was completed in 1755. Craik was one of the 'improving' landowners who transformed the Stewartry landscape during the eighteenth century.

He introduced new methods of drainage and crop rotation and helped improve the efficiency of agricultural machinery. This he did often against the wishes of his tenants, to whom he seemed a hard man. Craik also had a reputation as a drinker and a lothario; he sired a son by his sister-in-law, a Stewart of Shambellie. It was rumoured at the time of John Paul Jones' birth that the biological father was in fact Craik.

Craik was not the only remarkable member of the family. His daughter **Helen Craik** (1751-1825) was a writer of sentimental historical novels, and a correspondent of Robert Burns. The bard once called on her at Arbigland, an experience that the spinster may well have found challenging.

Helen was by no means immune, it seems, from disturbances of the heart. She reputedly fell in love with a groom employed on her father's estate. The social divide between them caused the relationship to be scandalous. One day the groom was found shot dead with a bullet to the head. It was officially accepted that either he had committed suicide or that the pistol had gone off when he fell from his horse. But locals suspected that he had been eliminated by a member of the laird's family, perhaps by William Craik himself.

Soon afterwards Helen left Arbigland, taking up residence directly across the Solway at Flimby, another family estate in Cumberland. She and her father became estranged. When he died, his property passed to a distant relative, even though Helen was his sole surviving legitimate child.

The gate piers at the entrance to the Arbigland estate are of interest because of who made them. They are the work of **Allan Cunningham** (1784-1842), a Dumfriesshire-born stonemason who went on to become an eminent man of letters within the London circle of Thomas de Quincey, Charles Lamb, William Hazlitt, John Keats and Thomas Hood.

Cunningham's poem *A Wet Sheet and a Flowing Sea* is still much anthologised. He had a facility in the writing of lyrics, and was so attuned to the style of the old Scottish ballads that he passed off some of his own compositions as traditional. It was while still a stonemason, working at Arbigland, that he met Jean Walker, whom he married and for whom he wrote *The Lovely Lass of Preston Mill:*

> Till death's cold dew-drop dims my eye,
> And my love-throbbing heart lies still;
> Thine every wish that warms my soul,
> My lovely lass of Preston Mill.

William Craik is thought to have had a hand in the design of Kirkbean **parish kirk**, the main part of which was completed in 1776. The striking tower was added in the 1830s. Inside there's a font presented in memory of John Paul Jones by United States Navy personnel who served in Britain during the Second World War.

The First World War memorial on the gateposts at the entrance to the kirkyard is unusual – it names not the dead but those who survived (the dead are commemorated elsewhere in the village).

The kirkyard has the gravestone of Paul Jones' father – 'erected by John Paul Junior', a reminder that Jones was a surname he adopted in later life.

Kirkbean School's **Millennium Cairn** has a sweet inscription:

> Thank you God for our school
> Made from granite stone
> Help us remember it forever
> When we are fully grown.

Kirkcudbright

Kirkcudbright was officially granted royal burgh status in 1455, but that was really only confirmation of what had for long been a reality, for the town was already being taxed as a trading centre by 1330.   The town is so ancient that no one can any longer know for certain how it got its name. It may have arisen from the twelfth-century 'Kirk of Cuthbert', whose site was where the town cemetery now is. Equally, the derivation may be from the Gaelic *caer cuabrit*, meaning 'fort on the bend of a river'. Or it may well have been that two separate linguistic strands met on common ground.

The capital of the Stewartry has one thing in common with the capital of Scotland: like Edinburgh, Kirkcudbright has antique beauty and status as the legislative centre but must concede that the *real* (economic) power lies elsewhere. Just as Glasgow is the commercial capital of Scotland, so the bigger and better placed Castle Douglas has the leading role within the Stewartry. It is characteristic of their difference that, when the Stewartry still had a railway system, Castle Douglas was on the main line, while out-of-the-way Kirkcudbright sat picturesquely at the end of a charming branch-line.

Kirkcudbright has another similarity with Edinburgh in having a medieval 'old town' and an eighteenth-century 'new town' (we

shall overlook its more recent bungaloid expansion).
The original settlement was
confined to not much more
than the present dog-
legged **High Street**. It was
built along a natural gravel
ridge and was easily defensible thanks to being almost
entirely surrounded by waterways and swamps. Entry
to the old town was by the
Water Yett [gate] at the
north end and the Meikle
Yett at the south-east. All

Kirkcudbright Station and the Free Kirk:
the station is now gone; the kirk is flats

classes of people were packed into this single L-shape. The properties facing onto the street belonged to the affluent, while the
poorer people lived down the closes. Today's frontages range in
age from the seventeenth century to the twentieth, though in some
cases foundations and back-walls are much older.

The main part of the **Tolbooth** – which functioned as a town hall,
a tax office and a jail – was built in the 1620s. The tower was
added in the 1640s, and the forestair – housing a cistern for the
public water supply - in the 1760s. In 1815 a replacement jail was
built across the road, and the present **Sheriff Court** was attached
to it in the 1860s: together, in their Victorian castellated romanti-
cism, they make a striking contribution to the town's skyline.

The Tolbooth - and not a car in sight!

Kirkcudbright

Kirkcudbright closes

Towards the end of the eighteenth century the overcrowding within the old town necessitated overspill, and so the 'new town' was laid out, with a spaciousness of the kind then in fashion. First came **Castle Street** in the 1790s, followed by **Union Street**. A creek running south from the harbour had to be filled in before the new **St Cuthbert Street** could proceed.

The modern spruceness of the **Moat Brae** belies its complicated history, a curious mix of the sacred and the secular. In the twelfth century it is likely to have been a 'motte' on which the Lords of Galloway had a timber castle in addition to their other base at Lochfergus north-east of the town.

In the 1450s the Franciscan Order – the 'Grey Friars' – built a priory church here. After Protestantism triumphed in the Reforma-

Greyfriars
Episcopal
Church

86

tion of the 1560s, part of the priory was retained as the parish kirk. The rest was demolished, the stone being used for the building of Maclellan's Castle (see below). The kirk was rebuilt in the 1730s, but by the 1830s the congregation had outgrown it and transferred to new premises, the present parish kirk.

The Moat Brae kirk was adapted into a school. Meanwhile, the area had also been developed commercially. To cope with the increasing volume of trade with the Baltic, the Basil Warehouse, complete with timber yard, was built here in the 1730s. There was also a shipyard. Towards the end of the nineteenth century the place had become a notorious eyesore, and, as part of a general clean-up, the redundant Basil Warehouse was demolished in 1895. In the early 1920s the school building was turned back into a place of worship, this time for the Episcopalians; the architect was Peter McGregor Chalmers, a big name at the time in the ecclesiastical field.

The present Greyfriars Episcopal Church incorporates the **Maclellan Monument**, a sumptuous Gothic/classical memorial for Sir Thomas Maclellan, builder of the castle across the road, and his second wife Grissel Maxwell. It was commissioned by their son Robert, who in 1633 was created Lord Kirkcudbright as a reward for his part in the Ulster 'plantations'. Thereafter the Maclellans appear to have exhibited a talent for squandering their resources, and the last Lord Kirkcudbright ended up selling gloves in Edinburgh in the early 1700s.

Maclellan's Castle is not really a castle at all but a fortified house, its military aspects more like decorative status-symbols. It was built in the 1580s for Sir Thomas Maclellan of Bombie, long-time Provost of Kirkcudbright. The builders had a ready supply of stone: Sir Thomas had acquired the right to strip most of the aban-

doned Franciscan priory. The Castledykes ruins (see below) were also used as an instant quarry. In scale the building was extraordinarily ambitious, so much so that Maclellan never finally paid all of his bills.

Maclellan's Castle

Sir Thomas would have been able to show it off in 1587 when King James VI visited and presented him with a silver gun as a prize 'to be shot for occasionally in order to accustom the leiges in the use of firearms'. By the mid-eighteenth century the castle was roofless. A nineteenth-century proposal to turn it into a prison was not pursued. The building, by then covered with ivy, was taken into public care in 1912.

By the time the developers came to lay out the final element of the 'new town' in the early years of the nineteenth century, the extra housing needs of the town had been largely satisfied, so in **St Mary Street** there is a concentration on prestigious commercial and civic buildings. The Renaissance-style splendour of the **Town Hall** was completed in 1879. An earlier version of 1863, called the Public Rooms, had to be demolished fourteen years after comple-

tion because of dodgy foundations. The new Town Hall housed the local museum until a dedicated building, the present **Stewartry Museum** – a riot of Scottish retro – was put up in 1892. The suave Bank of Scotland appeared in 1895. Across from the bank, the **parish kirk** (formerly St Cuthbert's) was built between 1836 and 1838.

The Stewartry Museum

At the north end of St Mary Street, an intriguing tale of Victorian philanthropy is attached to the construction in the 1870s of the square of small retirement homes now known as **Atkinson Place**. The minister of St Cuthbert's started receiving regular anonymous donations for the provision of 'almshouses'. The donor's identity was finally worked out only when the cessation of payments coincided with the death of Edward Atkinson, a local who had prospered as a banker in England. Another prosperous local, the merchant William Johnston, bequeathed funds for the building of the **Johnston 'Free' School**, completed in 1848 and enlarged in 1933.

The riverside area known as the **Castledykes** was the site of a castle built in the late 1200s. Its mound and surrounding ditches are still evident. Twentieth-century excavations revealed that the castle had been a substantial stone-built oblong with five towers. The site, looking straight down the estuary, would have been very

Plaque at
Castledykes

convenient for an early glimpse of any invading fleet. It appears to have been abandoned by the 1300s, but not before Edward I of England commandeered it during his occupation of south-west Scotland prior to the Wars of Independence.

Of all the many extraordinary characters associated over the centuries with Kirkcudbright, perhaps the most remarkable was **Billy Marshall**. Dubbed 'King of the Gypsies', he is now best remembered for the age he was thought to have been when he died in 1792 – one hundred and twenty!

Billy's gang of vagabonds, heavily involved in the smuggling trade, held sway over a large area of Galloway. In 1724 he was also among the leaders of the short-lived Levellers revolt against the landowners' enclosure of common land. According to Sir Walter Scott, he

Billy Marshall's grave, St Cuthbert's Cemetery

was lawfully married seventeen times, and even after reaching his century he was said to have sired at least another four illegitimate children. Some man! An obituarist wrote that, of all the thievish rogues operating in the county, 'he was by far the most honourable of his profession'.

Kirkcudbright

Kirkcudbright
Harbour
before 1910

As a **port**, Kirkcudbright has a long history, pre-dating anything mentioned so far. It is likely that the Romans, and later the Vikings, made use of this naturally sheltered berthing-place. When Edward I of England occupied the town in 1300, the fleet that sailed up the Dee consisted of 58 vessels and 1455 men. Before the coming of the railways and then motorised road transport, the town was by no means cut-off from the rest of the country. On the contrary: it was at the heart of the Solway/Irish Sea/Hebridean complex of sea-lanes, and Kirkcudbright ships regularly traded with continental Europe, the Americas and the Baltic.

The harbour as it is now took shape in 1910 when the nine-teenth-century dock (where the present Harbour Square is) was filled-in and a new quay built.

By the 1950s, however, the facility was practically moribund. David R Collin, chronicler of the town's maritime history, saw it for himself:

Scallop
boats at the
quay,
Kirkcudbright

...at low tide its muddy bottom supported rather more bicycles and bed-ends than it did boats. Vandals had not yet discovered shopping trolleys, so in those carefree days they threw each other into the water, attracted no doubt by untreated sewage which was all too evident at low tide in those bad old days.

Two developments brought a revival. In 1956 oil tankers began berthing to supply a storage depot (it closed in 1982). In the early 1960s, through the spirited initiative of John King, a Queenie scallop fishery was established, and today the greatly expanded fleet and the associated processing factory are major sources of employment.

At the harbour the wooden **sculpture** facing out to sea is by Charlie Easterfield and commemorates all who sailed from Kirkcudbright and never returned. For Kirkcudbright folk, loss of life at sea is not a thing of the past: in recent years two fishing-boats, the *Mhairi L* and *Solway Harvester,* have gone down and taken their crews with them.

With its ferro-concrete **bridge** across the Dee, completed in 1926, Kirkcudbright can fairly claim to have possibly the ugliest river-crossing in Scotland (the writer Dorothy L Sayers referred to its 'galumphing curves'). It has often been under threat of demolition. However, having formed the backdrop for so many paintings by Kirkcudbright artists, it is now a town icon, and, when the time finally comes for it to be replaced, it will probably have to be reproduced faithfully in all its original unsightliness. The Dee had to be crossed by ferry until 1868 when a metal swing-bridge came into service, the predecessor of the present structure.

The **Harbour Cottage Gallery** was opened in 1957. It was created out of a building that had been due for demolition, and is testimony to Kirkcudbright's renown, more past than present, as an artists' colony (see Part 2 - The Artists).

Kirkcudbright

Little Ross Island

At the mouth of Kirkcudbright Bay the lighthouse on **Little Ross Island** was completed in 1843 under the supervision of Robert Stevenson, grandfather of the writer Robert Louis. It was about to become automated in 1960 when a sensational murder took place on the island. Relief keeper Hugh Clark was shot dead by assistant keeper Robert Dickson. Convicted and sentenced to hang, Dickson was later reprieved of the noose, but took his own life with an overdose of pills at Saughton Prison in Edinburgh.

To the south of the town **St Mary's Isle** is now but a peninsula, though it used to be surrounded entirely by water at high tide. The earliest known building here was the Augustinian priory of Trail or Trellesholm, founded around 1200 by Fergus, Lord of Galloway, and dedicated to St Mary.

The mansion-house of the Earl of Selkirk was the scene in 1777 of John Paul Jones's daring raid (see Part 2 - The Pirate). The poet Robert Burns had 'a most happy evening' here in 1793 (see Part 2 - The Bards). The original house was demolished and replaced by another in the 1890s, which was itself destroyed by fire in 1940.

Although the Celtic-style granite Selkirk Memorial of 1885 at the corner of St Cuthbert Street and St Mary Street is for the sixth earl, the most interesting of the dynasty was in fact the fifth earl, **Thomas Douglas** (1771-1820). A political thinker with a radical outlook, he passionately believed that the best solution to the impoverishment of Highlanders was emigration, arguing the case in his book *Observations on the Present State of the Highlands of Scotland*. He put his beliefs into practice by founding two emigrant settlements in Canada, first on Prince Edward Island, later at Red River in Manitoba. His involvement with the Hudson Bay Company led its commercial rival, the Northwest Fur Company, to malign his work, and he spent much of the rest of his life defending his reputation. Ill and exhausted, he died at Pau in southern France during a recuperative trip, and was buried in the Protestant cemetery at Orthez.

Kirkgunzeon

Pronounced Kir-gunnion. The village is bisected by a burn, the Kirkgunzeon Lane, and the two parts are connected by an early-nineteenth-century bridge.

Kirkgunzeon Kirk

The **kirk** is of 1790, the manse of 1804. **Maxwell Memorial Hall** dates from 1906. The **mill** was once renowned for its oatmeal.

On the main Dalbeattie-Dumfries road, incorporated into a nineteenth-century farm steading, are the ruins of **Corra Castle**. The remains have been dated to the early-seventeenth century, but there must have been an earlier structure if, as is believed, Mary Queen of Scots spent a night here in 1568 after her defeat at the Battle of Langside (see Dundrennan).

North of the village is **Drumcoltran Tower** of about 1570. The words of wisdom in Latin above the entrance translate as: 'Keep hidden what is secret; speak little; be truthful; avoid wine; remember death; be pitiful.'

Drumcoltran Tower

Kirkpatrick Durham

This is a good example of a 'planned village' of the eighteenth century. It was the creation of the idealistic local minister, the **Rev David Lamont** (1753-1837). A Stewartry native, he was ordained at Kirkpatrick Durham in 1774.

With resources from an inheritance of land, he set about putting his enthusiasm for agricultural improvement and economic development into practice. The village was laid out around 1785. Within a few years there were some fifty properties, mainly for handloom weavers. By 1811 the population had risen to 1,150; there were seven inns and alehouses, and a horse racecourse. It was hoped to attract more substantial cloth-making industries, but the envisaged scale of expansion never materialised.

The Rev Lamont became a cleric of national repute. He was elected Moderator of the General Assembly of the Church of Scotland in 1822, the year of King George IV's infamous visit to Edinburgh; it was Lamont who preached before the King at St Giles' High Kirk. Around 1820 the house of **Durhamhill** was built for Lamont.

John Aitkenhead

Due west of the village is **Kilquhanity**, an 1820s house where, in 1940, John Aitkenhead (1910-1998) established his celebrated 'progressive' school along the lines of A S Neill's Summerhill. Aitkenhead – a wartime conscientious objector - had started his teaching career within the state system in Ayrshire, but rebelled against the educational establishment. Kilquhanity was based on his motto of *Liberty, Equality and Inefficiency* ('revolutions that are efficient,' he wrote, 'always end up killing people').

Of Kilquhanity School's early days, Aitkenhead said, 'We swallowed Neill hook, line and sinker; the children would have complete freedom to run the school'. He slightly tempered his views when, at the weekly school council meeting, the pupils voted to abolish bedtime. A former pupil recalled:

> We had our own farm with four cows, pigs and chickens. We smoked. There was a lot of teenage sex, a bit of dope, and we made rockets and bombs. We drank. I had a twelve-bore under my bed and God kept a pretty low profile. Instead of preachiness, there was a non-judgmental sense of community.

Kilquhanity

After an unfavourable inspectors' report, and with the building falling into disrepair, Aitkenhead decided to close the school in 1997. He died the following year, and, appropriately for a lifelong Scottish Nationalist, was buried in his kilt.

Due south of Kirkpatrick Durham is the clachan of **Old Bridge of Urr**. The bridge is indeed old, dating back to the late-sixteenth century. It was widened in 1772, and the parapets were re-built in 1843. The mill is of the late-eighteenth century.

Old Bridge
of Urr

Laurieston

This now quiet spot was once quite a significant junction of two important routes, one linking with Ayrshire in the north, the other crossing the south-west of Scotland between Dumfries and the ports for Ireland. Before the creation of Castle Douglas, it was the biggest settlement in the central Stewartry. Now only a single inn survives from its commercial heyday, and even the village school is defunct.

Laurieston was originally known as **Clachanpluck**. S R Crockett deplored the change:

> A certain name-changing fiend brought into our Erse and Keltic Galloway a number of mongrel names, probably some Laird Laurie with a bad education and a plentiful lack of taste, who, among other iniquities, called the ancient Clachan-of-Pluck after himself…

Little Duchrae

The defining Stewartry novelist, **Crockett** (1859-1914) was educated at the Free Kirk school here until moving to Castle Douglas at the age of seven. His early years were spent at **Little Duchrae** farm, three and a half miles to the north, a journey that the young Crockett did on foot. In later life he looked back upon his Little Duchrae upbringing with intense affection: 'Such a heavenly place for a boy to spend his youth in!'

The **Crockett Memorial** was erected in 1932 and opened by his widow, with the Galloway man of letters Sir Herbert Maxwell as the guest speaker. It is said that on one occasion when a passing bus-party had the memorial pointed out to them, some of the passengers exclaimed, 'Good old Davy!'

Unfortunately the memorial's inscription, incised onto a granite block, has the wrong year of birth, 1860 rather than 1859. The inscription continues:

TO THE MEMORY OF
SAMUEL RUTHERFORD
CROCKETT
AUTHOR OF THE RAIDERS
AND OTHER TALES OF GALLOWAY
A NATIVE OF THIS PARISH
24ᵀᴴ SEPT 1860 – 16ᵀᴴ APRIL 1914
A FAITHFUL SON AND CONSTANT LOVER
OF THAT GREY GALLOWAY LAND
WHERE ABOUT THE GRAVES OF THE MARTYRS
THE WHAUPS ARE CRYING
HIS HEART REMEMBERS NOW

A FAITHFUL SON AND CONSTANT LOVER
OF THAT GREY GALLOWAY LAND
WHERE ABOUT THE GRAVES OF THE MARTYRS
THE WHAUPS ARE CRYING
HIS HEART REMEMBERS HOW

The words echo the literary exchanges between Crockett and the exiled Robert Louis Stevenson – the two corresponded but never met in person. After Crockett sent RLS a copy of his first book, a collection of poems, Stevenson responded in verse:

Blows the wind to-day, and the sun and the rain are flying -
Blows the wind on the moors to-day and now,
Where about the graves of the martyrs the whaups are crying,
My heart remembers how!

Grey, recumbent tombs of the dead in desert places,
Standing stones on the vacant, wine-red moor,
Hills of sheep, and the howes of the silent vanished races,
And winds, austere and pure!

Be it granted me to behold you again in dying,
Hills of home! and to hear again the call -
Hear about the graves of the martyrs the pee-wees crying,
And hear no more at all.

Crockett continued the theme in his first book of stories, *The Stickit Minister* (1893), whose dedication reads:

To ROBERT LOUIS STEVENSON
of Scotland and Samoa, I dedicate these stories of that grey Galloway land where, about the graves of the Martyrs, the Whaups are crying – his heart remembers how.

(See Part 2 - The Novelists).

To the north of the village is **Laurieston Hall**, an Edwardian pile built round a seventeenth-century tower-house and set in 135 acres. In the 1950s it was used as an infectious diseases hospital. It was purchased in 1972 as a commune, an experiment in 'alternative' living which has proved to be remarkably enduring, so much so that some of the inaugural intake are now drawing their pensions.

Three of the original members financed the purchase from the sale of their London homes; ownership was subsequently transferred to a collective mortgage.

The two dozen or so members now have greater privacy in

their accommodation, though the living otherwise remains communal. Decisions are taken at a weekly meeting and everyone contributes to the work of the co-operative: growing fruit and vegetables; tending the hens, pigs and cows; gathering the vast amounts of firewood required for the heating and cooking systems.

The principles according to which they live appear not to be overly dogmatic: 'We believe in compost, laughing, wellies and freedom'.

West of Laurieston, off the road to Gatehouse of Fleet, is **Lochenbreck**, which in the nineteenth century was a well-known spa resort. There was a hotel for those seeking the reputedly curative qualities of the waters from its well, which were said to be useful 'in complaints of the stomach and disorders arising from obstruction and debility and they have often proved a very efficacious restorative, the water being transparent, a powerful tonic and diuretic and not unpleasant in taste'.

The spa's demise was much regretted. One commentator, writing during the First World War, stated:

> Since we are likely to avoid German spas for the next half century or longer, there is the more reason why that of Lochenbreck should be revived. The properties of the water are said to be valuable; the high moorland situation is splendid; motor-cars make it accessible; and the hotel would need little in the way of repair.

The proposal was never taken up.

Laurieston Hall

Lochfoot

The Dumfries and Galloway volume in *The Buildings of Scotland* series has a terse dismissal of Lochfoot: 'Undistinguished small village'. Poor Lochfoot.

Architectural historians, however, get rather more excited by **Hills Tower** to the south-east of the village. It is a pleasing combination of two buildings of different periods. The original four-storey tower-house was built for Sir John Maxwell, probably in the 1530s. Two centuries later a two-storey wing, in the early Georgian style, was added. These form one side of a courtyard which has a gatehouse of 1598.

Hills Tower

Lochrutton Kirk, now disused, was built in 1819. The Rev Henry Duncan, founder of the savings bank movement, was born at Lochrutton Manse in 1774.

Lochrutton Loch was the site of an Iron Age crannog.

Maxwelltown

Maxwelltown, being to the west of the River Nith, is historically a part of the Stewartry but has long been absorbed into Dumfries.

It was originally a small settlement called Brig-en - that is, at the west end of the old Devorgilla's Bridge across the Nith.

As Maxwelltown, it became a burgh in its own right in 1810. But it was so comprehensively subsumed into the urban sprawl of its neighbour to the east that the pretence of separateness was finally dropped in 1929.

Amalgamation of the two burghs had been electorally rejected in 1913 and 1927. But a postcard plebiscite was held in 1928 and this time the merger plan was approved by 1512 votes to 749.

The following year the two burghs were ceremoniously brought together across St Michael's Bridge. With schoolchildren lining the route and steeple bells ringing out, Provost O'Brien of Dumfries and Provost Brodie of Maxwelltown met at the centre of the bridge. That evening there was a grand fireworks display. Provost Brodie presided over the new greater burgh, followed equitably by a period of office for Provost O'Brien.

The Stewartry said a fond farewell.

Looking west over the medieval Devorgilla's Bridge into Maxwelltown

Minnigaff

Now in reality part of Newton Stewart in Wigtownshire, but, being on the east bank of the River Cree, very much belonging to the original Stewartry. It can claim seniority over its Cree-side neighbour into which it was inevitably absorbed. The 'new town of Stewart', created a Burgh of Barony in 1677 by landowner William Stewart, is an upstart by comparison with Minnigaff, which by then was already established as a market and as a fording place for the cattle-droving trade.

Curiously, Minnigaff's **parish kirk** retains the older Gaelic name of Monigaff. The present kirk is of the 1830s but beside it are the ruins of an earlier kirk, possibly of the seventeenth century. This may have been an ecclesiastical site from the thirteenth century.

Monigaff Parish Kirk   Monigaff Old Kirk

If Minnigaff folk might have complained about conceding their identity to Newton Stewart, the neighbouring and formerly separate community of **Creebridge** could just as well have felt the same towards Minnigaff to the north. Creebridge, like Minnigaff, just makes it into the original Stewartry by being on the right bank of the Cree.

The Cree Bridge

Minnigaff

The present bridge of its name, completed in 1813, was the first in the region to be built of local granite, though the masons had to be imported from Aberdeenshire.

The Creebridge/ Minnigaff area has several examples of **cairns** from two-three thousand years BC.

North-east from Minnigaff kirk is **Cumloden**, a former hunting lodge of the early 1820s which was converted into a home for the Earl of Galloway when in 1908, owing to depleted funds, the family had to vacate the grander Galloway House in Wigtownshire. It is not stately – architectural historians would describe it as a larger-scale *cottage orné* ['an artfully rustic small house associated with the Picturesque movement'].

Cumloden features in *An Unlikely Countess* (2004) by Louise Carpenter, the extraordinary story of the schizophrenic Randolph Stewart, 13th Earl of Galloway (born 1928), whose uninhibited behaviour made him such a family embarrassment that he was disinherited by his fearsome father. He married a working-class woman from the Borders, Lily Budge.

Lord Galloway, convinced that Lily had married Randolph for his money, saw money itself as the solution:

> 'How much would it take for an annulment?' he asked, flipping open his cheque book. Did he not realise, she protested, that she loved Randolph?
> 'It is not love you feel,' Lord Galloway told her, 'it is pity.'

North from Cumloden are the remains of the late-fifteenth/early-sixteenth-century **Garlies Castle**, an earlier Stewart residence.

Murray's Monument

North-east of Minnigaff, on the road to New Galloway, is **Murray's Monument**, commemorating the virtuoso linguist Alexander Murray (1775-1813). The precocious son of a Stewartry shepherd, he was largely self-taught in a whole range of languages.

Murray was still only eighteen when he embarked on a major translation from German of Arnold Drackenburg's lectures on Roman authors. His talent was spotted and he was encouraged to go to university. He entered Edinburgh University in 1793, having impressed the academic authorities with his knowledge of Homer, Horace, the Hebrew psalms and French.

As well as languages, he also studied divinity, and would later practise for a time as a Church of Scotland minister at Haugh of Urr.

He continued accumulating linguistic knowledge, moving on to Asian and African languages. In 1811 a diplomatic message from Abyssinia, written in Ethiopic, arrived in London for King George III. The Government turned to Murray as the only competent translator.

In 1812 he was appointed Professor of Oriental Languages in Edinburgh but died of consumption just months later. His widow was supported by a government pension in recognition of his work on that Abyssinian letter. His pioneering study, *History of the European languages, or, Researches into the affinities of the Teutonic, Greek, Celtic, Slavonic, and Indian nations* was published posthumously.

Murray's monument was erected in 1835 opposite his boyhood home at the farm of Dunkitterick.

East of Minnigaff, **Kirroughtree** is an estate and house developed by generations of the Heron family – many of them, confusingly, called Patrick. The house, now a hotel, was completed in 1719, but has had numerous additions at various times.

The best known **Patrick Heron** (died 1803) was an acquaintance of the poet Robert Burns, who visited Kirroughtree in 1794. Burns, with some misgivings, helped Heron become a Westminster MP by twice writing an election ballad for his campaign. Heron was fortunate to have been rehabilitated into public life, for twenty years earlier he had been partly responsible for a wave of bankruptcies that sent the Stewartry economy into depression. He was a partner in the Ayr-based bank Douglas, Heron & Company. It collapsed in 1773 through, according to a historian of Scottish banking, 'giving credit too easily; ignorance of the principles of business; and carelessness or iniquity of officers'. Its shareholders, many of them local, were liable for the debts and were, as a result, financially wiped out.

Kirroughtree House Hotel

Mossdale

The name 'Mossdale' does not sound Stewartry-esque. The novelist S R Crockett, who spent part of his childhood near here, bemoaned in the early years of the twentieth century the anglicisation of old Gaelic names in these parts, castigating the land-owning class for changing, for example, Loch Grenoch to Woodhall Loch:

> Farther afield we have a crop, happily thin sown and soon fading away, of Summerhills, Parkhills, Willowbanks, and such like – of which that to be most regretted is the merging of the ancient name of the Duchrae estate in that of the mansion-house of Hensol, a word which has no historical connection with Galloway, but merely preserves a souvenir of the early youth of a late proprietor. But Woodhall Loch (after you have become accustomed to the barbarism) smells as sweet, and its water ripples as freshly as ever did that of Loch Grenoch – which at least is some comfort.

(Crockett had the same point to make about the village further south where he had his early education – see Laurieston). The big house of **Hensol** which he mentions was erected in the 1820s and was built of granite in a 'Tudor' style as non-native as its re-naming.

Tiny, tranquil Mossdale once had great steam trains not only passing through but also stopping. It had its very own **railway station** on the 'Paddy' main line, though it was officially named New Galloway station. It fell under the 'Beeching Axe' of the mid-1960s.

Mossdale was the point from which west-bound trains entered the wild and dramatic landscape that gave this route such romantic resonance for steam-railway buffs. From Mossdale the next sta-tion westwards was the extremely remote **Loch Skerrow**. At first there was no halt here. But a

Looking west from Mossdale along the old railway line

small community of railway maintenance workers and their fami-lies developed, and for them – the wives going shopping to Castle Douglas, the children attending school in Mossdale - a short wooden platform was built. Since Loch Skerrow was popular with fishermen, they too were picked up and dropped off, but it was always unofficial until, out of the blue in 1955, Loch Skerrow finally appeared in the timetable as a recognised stop.

To the north of Mossdale is the eastern entrance to the **Raiders' Road**, a ten-mile forest drive along the Black Water of Dee to Clat-teringshaws in the west. The route follows part of an old drove-road featured in S R Crockett's most famous tale of the Galloway hills, *The Raiders*.

Mossdale is one of the main ac-cess-points for the **Galloway Kite Trail**. It was here in 2003 that the trail was officially launched. It is part of a nationwide programme for re-introducing the red kite, a bird of prey which by the 1950s had been reduced to a small presence in Wales. According to the Royal So-ciety for the Protection of Birds, the

red kite – a scavenger regarded in some quarters as vermin - has been subject for centuries to 'intensive human persecution'. The trail is centred mainly on the Loch Ken area; it includes outdoor viewing-points, hides and a feeding-station.

New Abbey

The abbey was 'new' because the Cistercians already had one at Dundrennan. Referred to by the monks as either 'Douz Coeur' (Norman French) or 'Dulcis Cor' (ecclesiastical Latin), it is now known to us as **Sweetheart Abbey** in recognition of the great love-story that lay behind its thirteenth-century origins. It is a fabulously wealthy widow's memorial to her husband, whose heart she had had removed from his body, embalmed and placed in an ivory casket which she carried with her for the rest of her life. In 1289 or 1290 when she died, her 'sweet, silent companion' was buried along with her inside the abbey.

The widow was **Dervorguilla**, daughter of Alan, Lord of Galloway. The husband was John de Balliol, descendent of Anglo-Norman immigrants who built Barnard Castle in County Durham. Through inheritance on both sides, this illustrious couple became multinational magnates, with land and property throughout Scotland, Ireland, both northern and southern England and France. Their youngest son, incidentally, was briefly and miserably King of Scotland (see Part 2 - The Early History).

In Dervorguilla's time it was not uncommon for widows of means to make some kind of religious endowment in memory of their late husbands: a chapel annex perhaps or, more modestly, a candle fund for the poorer supplicants. That was not good enough

Sweetheart Abbey

for Dervorguilla. In the public expression of her grief there were to be no half-measures; the gesture would be no less than a whole monastery, to be built from scratch at enormous cost. She also lavished money on carrying through John's wish to found a scholars' hall in Oxford, and Balliol College was the result.

Dervorguilla decided to establish the abbey soon after John's death in 1268 or 1269. By 1270 a site inspection was being carried out by the abbots of Furness and Rievaulx on the orders of the Cistercian authorities. They found it to be ideal for their monastic way of life. It was sufficiently secluded to provide them with the right conditions for a life of prayer founded on piety, austerity and chastity.

But the Cistercians were also highly practical men who believed in making the most of their assets. They were particularly skilled as farmers, breeding sheep, cattle and horses, and fully engaging in the wool trade.

The site had many advantages. It was sheltered to the west by the massive granite hulk of Criffel and was level and fertile, with plentiful sources of water both for drinking and for their fishponds. To the east and south lay the sea: the calm waters of the Nith opening into the Solway Firth giving access to the whole western seaboard.

On the 10[th] of April 1273 Dervorguilla signed the charter of foundation. By this stage, two of her eight children had already died, and they too were included in the list of people to be prayed for in perpetuity:

> ...for the souls of John Bal[l]iol the grantor's lord and late spouse, Hugh his son and hers, Cecilia her daughter, the grantor's own soul, and those of all their ancestors and successors and of all faithful Christians.

The abbey was to be financed with the proceeds from two gifted parishes: Lochkinderloch (the old name for New Abbey itself), and Kirkpatrick Durham 20 miles to the west. It was to be run as a 'daughter' of the earlier Cistercian establishment at Dundrennan near Kirkcudbright, a foundation of Dervorguilla's great-grandfather and the first Lord of Galloway, Fergus.

The design and layout of Sweetheart are similar to Dundrennan's. The main structure was cruciform: a six-bay nave to the west, a choir with the high altar plus a further presbytery to the east, and between them the crossing with north and south transepts. To the south lay the administrative and living quarters.

Building work began with the clearing of the site. Granite boulders were removed and re-cycled in the making of the sturdy pe-

New Abbey around 1910

rimeter wall. Remaining granite rubble was used as in-fill for the walling of the main buildings. Red sandstone, shipped across the River Nith from Dumfriesshire in the east, was the facing material.

What might Dervorguilla have seen of her grandiose scheme before she died around 1290? By then almost certainly the choir, the crossing and the transepts were complete, plus a substantial part of the nave. After her death and burial by the high altar, work came to a halt. The project became a casualty of the political and military turbulence of the next forty years or so. By the end of the Scottish War of Independence the abbey was in a sorry state of disrepair, and it was not until later in the fourteenth century that construction could be resumed, this time under the patronage of a new-style Lord of Galloway, Archibald The Grim (see Part 2 - The Early History).

In the late-sixteenth century, attempts by the zealots of the Reformation to close down the abbey met fierce resistance from the last abbot, **Gilbert Broun**. He simply refused to budge and, in the words of his opponents, continued 'enticing his people to papistry'. To avoid arrest, he escaped to France, but was soon back and up to his old tricks again. Finally, a Protestant delegation arrived, battered his door down and held a public burning of all his belongings, not least his 'popische trasche'. He was imprisoned in Blackness Castle on the Firth of Forth and, on his release, again fled to France, where he died around 1612.

The Reformers adapted the abbey refectory into their new kirk. Then another kirk was built within the precincts in 1731. The rest of the abbey buildings became a handy quarry. In 1779 a group of locals bought the ruins, with the intention of conserving them. But in 1852 a government inspector reported that there was 'no evidence of any recent attempts having been made for the preservation of the interesting remains'. Repairs were carried out in the 1860s and the parish kirk was removed in 1877 (the year the present parish kirk was completed), but it was not until 1928 that the site was taken into state care.

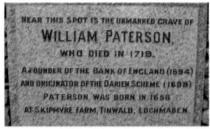

NEAR THIS SPOT IS THE UNMARKED GRAVE OF
WILLIAM PATERSON,
WHO DIED IN 1719.

A FOUNDER OF THE BANK OF ENGLAND (1694)
AND ORIGINATOR OF THE DARIEN SCHEME (1698)
PATERSON WAS BORN IN 1658
AT SKIPMYRE FARM, TINWALD, LOCHMABEN.

The cemetery beside the Abbey contains, in an unmarked grave, the remains of **William Paterson** (1658-1719), the Scotsman (born in Dumfriesshire) who is credited with having founded the Bank of England in 1694. Paterson was a successful London merchant but lost a fortune in the ill-fated attempt to found a Scottish colony at Darien on the Isthmus of Panama.

The construction of **Shambellie House** (now the National Museum of Costume) was a shambles. It began in 1856 and went on till 1860 – double the time it should have taken. The architect was David Bryce, an eminent exponent of the revivalist Baronial style that was so fashionable in Victorian Scotland.

Compared with the grand scale on which Bryce was used to working, a small country house in the Stewartry was rather beneath him. He came bitterly to regret having taken on the project, for in William Stewart he had a client whose penny-pinching and pernickitiness led to a stream of complaints to Bryce's Edinburgh office.

Misunderstandings between the two of them and their various contractors were compounded by mishaps. The worst setback came in the winter of 1856-7. The ship bringing a consignment of roof slates sank in the Solway Firth. Both cargo and crew were lost. The sarking which had already been laid across the roof timbers conducted rainwater into the wall masonry, flushing out the pointing and causing settlement that left sills and lintels cracked. In despair the client's wife wrote to the architect:

Shambellie House

109

New Abbey

> Mr Stewart is so much annoyed and disgusted with the state of the house that I cannot prevail upon him again to write you on the subject. Now out of consideration not only for the furniture but for the health of the family I am reduced to trouble you and to beg that something may immediately be done to prevent the rain completely destroying the house.

The house was eventually completed but Stewart held back money owed for it, and the dispute ended up in court. Stewart was forced to pay up. He had wanted a house for £2000. By the end he calculated that it had cost £2984 – and that did not include all the legal fees.

The late-eighteenth-century **Corn Mill**, restored to full working-order and in the care of Historic Scotland, is a popular attraction.

The Corn Mill

New Abbey today abounds with well-preserved old things to look at, and not all of them are on the level: the hilltop edifice to the west is the **Waterloo Monument**, erected soon after the 1815 battle and paying tribute to the valour not just of the British troops but also of the Belgians and Prussians.

The Waterloo Monument

Sadly, there is one aspect of its heritage in which New Abbey appears to take no pride. Its people have apparently been beguiled into the heretical belief that they belong to Dumfriesshire. They will be forgiven if they return to the fold of the Stewartry (see Introduction).

New Galloway

The main street and Town Hall

How can there be a New Galloway in Galloway? Answer: when it became a royal burgh in 1633, its name was the *Newtown of Galloway*. Its proudest boast has always been that it is the smallest royal burgh in Scotland. Despite its size, it had at one time the full panoply of town government: a provost, four baillies, a dean of guild, a treasurer and twelve councillors. All of that was swept away in Scotland's local government reorganisation of 1974. The **Town Hall** of 1875 is a reminder of its civic heyday.

To the south of the present town, **Kenmure Castle** is the key to New Galloway's original development. The mound on which it sits at the top of Loch Ken is probably artificial and had almost certainly been built upon since medieval times. The present structure, now dangerously ruinous, was begun towards the end of the sixteenth century by the Gordons of Lochinvar; added to in the seventeenth century; and further altered in the nineteenth century. It was abandoned in the twentieth century; a fire destroyed its interior around 1950.

It was the first Viscount Kenmure, John Gordon (1599?-1634), who acquired the royal charter authorising the creation of a burgh. He had planned a development for nearby Dalry but, following a disagreement with the locals, a site to the north of the castle was chosen instead, and so New [town of] Galloway came into being.

The first Viscount and his wife Jane were passionate supporters of the famous Covenant minister Samuel Rutherford (see Anwoth). They became close friends. Rutherford attended the Viscount on his death-bed, and wrote an account of his passing, *The Last and Heavenly Speeches and Glorious Departure of John, Viscount Kenmure* (1649). More of Rutherford's published letters were to the Viscountess than to any of his other correspondents. When she became depressed after the death of yet another infant

New Galloway

Aerial view of Kenmure Castle

Aerial view of Kenmure Castle

girl, Rutherford's celebrated advice to her was:

> She is only sent on before, like unto a star which, going out
> of sight, doth not die and vanish, but still shineth in another
> hemisphere.

The Kenmure dynasty later aligned itself with the Jacobite cause, for which William Gordon, the sixth Viscount, was beheaded at Tower Hill in London in 1716. At his trial he begged for mercy as 'the means to keep my Wife and Four Small Children from starving; the thoughts of which, with my Crime, makes me the most Unfortunate of all Gentlemen'. The poet Robert Burns reworked a Jacobite song about him:

> O Kenmure's on and awa, Willie,
>   O Kenmure's on and awa;
> An' Kenmure's Lord's the bravest Lord
>   That ever Galloway saw.

The song was published in 1792, and in the following year, on a tour through the Stewartry, Burns stayed with the Jacobite Kenmure's grandson, the seventh Viscount, for three days (see Part 2 - The Bards).

The scale of the original plan for New Galloway's development never materialised, mainly because its promoter, the first Viscount, died the year after the burgh charter was granted. Instead it modestly lived off its convenience as a stopover point on the Old Edinburgh Road for pilgrims visiting St Ninian's shrine at Whithorn. It also became central to the cattle trade: it was on the route for the drovers heading for England, it had its own cattle market and became the location for the early agricultural shows of the Glenkens. Its communications were greatly enhanced in the early 1820s by

The Ken Bridge

the building of the **Ken Bridge**. Previously the only way across this stretch of the River Ken was by ford or ferry, but in full spate the river was fearsomely obstructive. There had been campaigning for a bridge from the 1750s, and no less than four attempts at creating one ended in the foundations being swept away by the torrent. At last the great engineer John Rennie (1761-1821) came up with an elegant solution. His sturdy structure, made of local granite, has five arches rising well above the floodplain.

Kells parish kirk was built at the northern edge of the burgh around the same time as the Ken Bridge was being constructed. Its graveyard, like others in the Glenkens, contains striking examples of Covenanter memorials – and also a touching carved tribute to a gamekeeper, written by the kirk minister:

> Ah John, what changes since I saw thee last;
> Thy fishing and thy shooting days are past.
> Bagpipes and hautboys thou canst sound no more
> Thy nods, grimaces, winks and pranks are o'er.
> Thy harmless, queerish incoherent talk,
> Thy wild vivacity and trudging walk
> Will soon be quite forget. Thy joys on earth,
> A snuff, a glass, riddles and noisy mirth,
> Are vanished all. Yet blest, I hope thou art,
> For in thy station weel thou playdst thy part.

To the south-west **Auchencloy** is where in 1684 Graham of Claverhouse and his government troops surprised eight Covenanters, killing four of them on the spot. In 1835 a conventicle was held here to raise funds for a memorial, which was subsequently built in granite. The name of James McMichael was misspelt, an error that was corrected in 2006 by the Scottish Covenanter Memorials Association. Reverence for these 'martyrs' to the Presbyterian cause still burns four centuries later.

Palnackie

This backwater on the River Urr once fairly bustled with **shipping**. It was the port for land-locked Castle Douglas. The present, largely disused Barlochan Basin was constructed with wooden piles in the 1850s. Unfortunately, within a decade the railway had reached Castle Douglas and thus began Palnackie harbour's steady decline, though it continued in use for the export of granite from the nearby Craignair quarry. During the Second World War barges brought explosives supplies for the Edingham factory on the outskirts of Dalbeattie. A short distance up-river was another berthing point, Garden Basin at the foot of the Garden Burn. Palnackie was previously known as Gardenburn.

All that remains of a once-busy port

The local **granite** was the main building material for the older village houses. The mock-castellated Barlochan House was built towards the end of the nineteenth century.

Palnackie's modern claim to fame is the annual **flounder-tramping** festival, in which competitors wade through the mud off the South Glen peninsula and have to catch flounders with their toes. The festival, held in early August, started in 1971, the original motive having been to raise funds for the Royal National Lifeboat Institution.

To the south of the village is the late-fifteenth-century **Orchardton Tower**, the only example from this period in Scotland of a cylindrical design. Round towers were common in Ireland, so Orchardton's builder, John Cairns, may have had Irish connections. The tower was the laird's principal private accommodation. To the south and west are the remains of servants' quarters and workshops.

Orchardton Tower

Palnure

Apart from a milk products factory, modern Palnure ('stream of the yews') seems to have little to offer. But in the nineteenth century it was a busy wee place. Dotted along the east bank of the Palnure Burn were **lead mines**, whose products, along with grain and timber, were exported from a small harbour.

Hill climbers will find that the best route for **Cairnsmore of Fleet** is accessed from Palnure.

In 1980 a United States Air Force helicopter lifted to the summit a granite memorial for the two dozen of so airmen, of various nationalities, who have fatally crashed on Cairnsmore. Most of the victims were trainee pilots flying out of RAF Wigtown. The first crash was in August 1940 when a German Heinkel was returning from laying mines in Belfast Lough.

Palnure has another connection with aviation. Cairnsmore House, to the north-east, was home to **'The Flying Duchess'**, Mary Du Caurroy (1865-1937), wife of the 11th Duke of Bedford. It was not until 1926, when she was sixty, that she flew for the first time. She had been told that changes in air pressure would relieve the tinnitus from which she suffered for most of her life.

She fell in love with flying and took lessons, finally gaining her pilot's licence in 1933. She and a co-pilot broke records for flights to India and South Africa. When she flew herself north from the main family seat at Woburn Abbey, she would land in a field near Cairnsmore House, having 'buzzed' her pals at Cardoness and Cassencarie on the way.

Her end came in a flying accident: she came down off the east coast of England and, apart from odd bits of wreckage, no trace of her was ever found.

The Duchess's only child, a son who later became the 12th Duke of Bedford (1888-1953), was born at Cairnsmore House, and spent much of the Second World War here. A devout Christian, he registered as a conscientious objector. He participated prominently in pacifist campaigns but his reputation was tainted by association with pro-German groups. He was considered fortunate not to have been interned.

Parton

FLOREAT·PARTONA

L et Parton Flourish - asserts the Latin motto at the entrance to the cute village hall of 1908. We should not be surprised by this learned touch, for Parton is proud of its connection with a man of great learning, the experimental physicist James Clerk Maxwell, whose pioneering thinking on light, sound, electromagnetism and colour led directly to the development of radio, television, radar and satellite communication. Clerk Maxwell is buried in Parton kirkyard and the village makes much of this fact, but the great man's closer association is with Corsock, so his full story can be found elsewhere (see Corsock).

Parton's architectural centrepiece, stretching along one side of the main road through the village, is the curved row of twee 'Arts & Crafts' **cottages** with wooden doorway canopies. At the northern end of the row, with its distinctive wood-clad clock-tower, is the former communal laundry. Another communal facility, in the back-garden and now converted into a summerhouse, was the octagonal set of outside loos – the famous **Parton Privy**.

The whole development was conceived as a 'model village' by the benevolent occupier of Parton House (demolished in 1964), a Manchester manufacturer called Benjamin Rigby Murray, who bought an estate here in 1852. He did not live to see his tenants' enjoyment of their quaint new homes. The scheme was completed in 1901, and a memorial plaque describes it as 'the last act of a kindly life'. In the following year the locals again showed their appreciation by erecting a granite fountain – 'in grateful remembrance of their friend'.

Another plaque, erected by the Association for the Preservation of Rural Scotland, pays tribute to the builder whose later reconstruction of the village 'saved it from extinction'.

Parton's architectural showpiece

Parton

Apart from the Clerk Maxwell mausoleum, the grounds of the **parish kirk** (1830s) are worth visiting for the view over the wall of an eleventh- or twelfth-century earthwork described by one historian as 'the best-looking 'Christmas-pudding'-shaped motte in Galloway'. The kirkyard also contains the ruins of an earlier kirk, believed to date from the 1590s.

Parton kirkyard

Parton today may seem remote, but for a century it enjoyed excellent communication with the rest of the country. It was fortunate to have its own **railway station** on the great line across Galloway from Castle Douglas to the Wigtownshire coast, which opened in 1862. The former station is now a private house.

A short distance north of the village the line took a dramatic sweep westwards, crossing Loch Ken at Boat o' Rhone on a wrought-iron and sandstone viaduct, a heroic piece of Victorian engineering which still stands, albeit precariously. At this point the railway left behind the gentle gradients of the Dee valley and entered the wilds romantically associated with Richard Hannay's adventures in John Buchan's *The Thirty-Nine Steps* (see Part 2 - The Novelists).

As a wistful reminder of rural public transport in its pre-'Beeching Axe' heyday, let us consult a 1920s Bradshaw's railway timetable. We discover that there were no fewer than three daily southbound departures from Parton (Sundays being excepted of course) that would have taken you, with changes at Dumfries and Carlisle, to London Euston in good time. The 0945 arrived at 1830, the 1121 at 2230; and, if you didn't mind slumming it on the milk train, you could have taken the 1739 arriving at 0500.

Loch Ken Viaduct

Rhonehouse

O nce better known as Keltonhill, and long famous for its **an-nual fair**, held on the first Tuesday after the 17th of June.

When you see how many roads converge at the square (actually a triangle), you can understand how Keltonhill developed into a gathering-place. Robert Heron reported on the fair in his account of a tour through south-west Scotland in 1792:

> From Ireland, from England, and from the most distant parts of North Britain, horse-dealers, cattle-dealers, sellers of sweetmeats, and of spiritous liquors, gypsies, pick-pockets, and smugglers are all accustomed to resort to this fair. Every house in the village is crowded; and all are become, upon this occasion, houses of entertainment. Through the whole fair-day, one busy, tumultuous scene is exhibited of bustling backwards and forwards, bargaining, wooing, carousing, quarrelling.

In his *Scottish Gallovidian Encyclopedia* (1824) John Mactaggart extolled the sense of fun:

> While the scenes thicken, the tents get crowded; whisky is skilted over like whey; bonny lasses are to be met, who cling round one like binwud [woodbine]; and who would not cling to them in turn, sweet souls?

Billy Marshall, 'king of the gypsies' who is reputed to have lived to the age of 120, prided himself on never missing a Keltonhill Fair. Even when soldiering on the Continent, it is said, somehow he used to manage back home for the occasion (see Kirkcudbright).

The local contributor to the 1790s *Statistical Account of Scotland* was alarmed to find four inns, and worse still:

> ...many small tippling places. These little gin-shops have a ruinous effect, upon the health and the morals of the lower classes of the people...

The fair flourished until about 1860. The livestock trading gradually re-located to Castle Douglas. But Rhonehouse continued to be a bustling place well into the twentieth century. In the early part of the century there were three blacksmiths, a saddler, two cobblers, three grocers and a tailor with three employees.

By the 1960s, however, the *Statistical Account of Scotland* was reporting a sense of nostalgia:

> The people of the village still talk of the fair, and even refer to the several houses that remain and once were inns, though these days are well beyond living memory. This village was destined to lose its glory.

It was here at Keltonhill/ Rhonehouse, during the fair of 1723, that the **Levellers** were formed. This was not a local folk-music group but a peasants' revolt against the loss of common grazing rights. Their target was the programme of drystane-dyke building which the landowners had inaugurated to enclose their land for the benefit of the cattle trade. Possibly fortified by supplies of Keltonhill Fair beverages, an initial group of the dispossessed set off from here and, gathering support along the way, embarked on a dyke-destroying rampage through the county (see Part 2 - The Land and the Sea).

Ringford

Neilson's Monument

The hilltop pyramid overlooking Ringford is **Neilson's Monument**. It commemorates James Beaumont Neilson (1792-1865), inventor of the hot-blast method of iron smelting. The profits from his patent enabled him to buy and retire to the Queenshill estate north of the village.

Born at Shettleston in Glasgow, Neilson was apprenticed in the coal industry and then joined Glasgow's first gasworks, becoming managing director. He invented the 'swallow-tail' gas burner. But it was when he turned his attention to the iron industry that he made his most significant contribution to the Industrial Revolution. The original smelters had blasted the furnace with cold air. Neilson successfully proved that hot air was more effective

He patented his invention in 1828, though he spent many years defending his rights through the courts. The hot-blast method hugely increased productivity, tripling the output per ton of coal and enabling the use of inferior fuel.

Neilson retired from the gasworks in 1847 and came to live at Queenshill in 1851, swapping the industrial fug of central Scotland (to which his inventiveness had contributed) for the fresh air and tranquillity of life as a Stewartry land-owner.

His son became a well-known Glasgow locomotive manufacturer whilst also enjoying life as a Stewartry 'laird' and it was this son – Walter Montgomerie Neilson – who in 1883 commissioned the hilltop obelisk in recognition of his father's achievement.

It is a sturdy but pleasingly understated structure made from local whinstone and granite – impressive in its minimalist ruggedness. There are no florid testimonials of the kind that the Victorians usually favoured - just a simple, bald statement in capital letters which, as you arrive at the summit, looks like a newspaper headline:

NEILSON
HOT BLAST
1828

On the opposite side is an equally succinct inscription:

1883 W.M.N. FECIT [Latin – *did, made*]

Ringford

'Hot Blast' Neilson and the inscription on his monument.

'Hot Blast' Neilson's grandson, also Walter Montgomerie, founded in 1903 the **Tarff Valley Agricultural Co-operative Society**, the first of its kind in Scotland. He saw that bulk-buying would be to the benefit of his tenant-farmers. Coal and lime were brought by rail to Tarff station on the Castle Douglas-Kirkcudbright line.

The society's first base was a tin shed at the station road-end. Since the railway closed in the mid-1960s it has occupied the whole station site, and now trades as Tarff Valley Ltd on a scale far removed from its charmingly homespun early days, as this extract from its official history demonstrates:

> The first vehicle belonging to the Society was the Secretary's bicycle in 1921. In 1924, one customer thought that there was no need for a telephone in the office - the public telephone box on the other side of the road would suffice; whilst in 1927 the Tongland and Twynholm Ploughing Association received 5 stones of flour, as a prize for the competitor with the largest family.

Fellend Farm, to the north of Ringford, was home to **John Morrison** (1782-1853), painter, poet, literary dilettante and, curiously, also a land-surveyor. Morrison was born in the parish of Terregles in the eastern Stewartry and brought to Fellend as a boy.

His family were farming folk, and from time to time in a varied and unsettled career he himself tried making a living from the land. His aspirations, however, went higher. He attracted the attention of the 5th Earl of Selkirk who paid for him to be trained in Edinburgh as a land-surveyor with a view to employing him on his colonial initiatives. But, while in the capital, Morrison took the opportunity to pursue his artistic bent under the tutorship of the landscape and portrait painter Alexander Nasmyth. The earl, calling on him in Edinburgh while he was out, was horrified by what he found:

I was disappointed to observe the arrangement of your studies. Instead of books of science, I found Shakespeare, Ossian, and other stuff. I even saw a violin and books of music. What have you to do with such trumpery? A lad like you, fighting for his existence, ought to mind nothing but the sternly useful. Let me advise you to let these trifling amusements occupy as little of your time as possible.

Morrison further offended his patron by rejecting his offer of employment abroad. He spent the rest of his life making a precarious living from his various skills. He got to know the civil engineer Thomas Telford when he was working on the Tongland Bridge project, and was employed by Telford on a number of surveying assignments, including a proposed railway line between Glasgow and Berwick. He also worked for the engineer John Rennie. But he grew to dislike a profession 'that requires neither much imagination

John Morrison

nor taste', and tried to make it as a painter, without any great success. He also fancied himself as a poet. *Poems of John Morrison* was published in 1832. In one of his works a young woman drowns herself in the River Nith when she discovers that her betrothed has switched his allegiance to a woman with money:

Now mark the cursed love for gold:
A lady came into that land,
And for a lover rather old,
Yet she had money at command.
I wish that we could pass it over,
And not on human frailty dwell,
But true, alas! this faithless lover
In love wild with the stranger fell;
And he has hurried to his trunk,
Pack'd and return'd the correspondance
Of this poor maid, who thereby sunk,
Beyond all hope, in deep despondance.

His book, perhaps not surprisingly, did not sell well.

Morrison was notorious for his arrogant dogmatism and acid wit, and his tongue was not inhibited by the presence of superior intellects. 'So great was the vanity of Morrison,' according to one commentator, 'that even Sir Walter Scott was not allowed to pass uncontradicted'. In the company of the Scotts, Morrison sneered at the Wilkie group portrait, *The Abbotsford Family*. Scott's daughter Anne put him in his place: 'Oh, I forgot, Mr Morrison, you are a painter yourself, and I have often heard it remarked that there is no friendship in trade, but I never saw it verified before'. 'The Ettrick Shepherd', poet James Hogg, described Morrison's pretensions thus: 'Of peasant make, and doubtful mein,/ Affecting airs of high disdain.'

Morrison was buried in Tongland kirkyard.

Kirkconnel Moor, north-west of Ringford, is a totemic site in the annals of the anti-Episcopalian Covenanters movement. It was here on the 20th February 1685, during the 'Killing Times', that five supporters of the cause were discovered by government troopers under the command of the notorious Grierson of Lag. John Bell, David Halliday, Andrew McRobert, James Clement and Robert Lennox were shot on the spot. Grierson ordered their bodies to be left where they fell.

Four of them were later taken away for burial by friends. The fifth, James Clement, who was not local, was buried on the moor. A gravestone marks the spot.

In 1831 a granite obelisk was erected in memory of all five 'martyrs'. An estimated 10,000 people attended a ceremonial service. Its centenary was celebrated in 1931 by a service attended by some 6,000. In 1985 there was another gathering, this time to acknowledge the three-hundredth anniversary of the massacre. On that occasion, the size of the congregation was in three rather than four figures – but the very fact that this latter-day 'conventicle' took place so long after the original killings demonstrates the Stewartry's abiding attachment to the notion of religious freedom.

South of Ringford, close to the A75's junction with the road to Kirkcudbright, the building sitting rather forlornly on a hillock is the former **Tarff Valley Free Kirk**, a reminder of the civil war that broke out within the Church of Scotland in the 1830s, the so-called 'Ten Year Conflict' that culminated in The Disruption of 1843.

As ever in kirk matters, the arguments were dense and complicated. Basically, it was a controversy over patronage, the extent to which the State and the landowners should have a say in the appointment of ministers. The Evangelicals in the General Assembly believed that the Kirk was no longer 'free', so in 1843 one third of them left the Kirk and established the Free Kirk under the charismatic leadership of the Rev Thomas Chalmers. The new organisation expensively replicated all the facilities of the 'established' one: kirks, manses and schools. After the two sides eventually reunited in 1929 there was a surplus of infrastructure, evidence of which can still be seen in many Stewartry towns and villages.

Rockcliffe

O nce upon a time an ordinary wee place – a settlement of fishermen, quarrymen, copper miners and, of course, smugglers. Then it was discovered by the Victorians and Edwardians as a **seaside resort**. The coming of the railways increased its accessibility. It became relatively easy to journey by train from Glasgow to Dalbeattie and then by charabanc down to the coast. Many of the substantial houses along the sea-front were put up during this period. The Baron's Court Hotel was built in the early 1880s specifically to serve the holiday trade. However, Rockcliffe's development was never of the candy-floss and fish-and-chips variety. The village's clientele tended always towards the genteel, as do its present-day inhabitants – largely affluent retirees of the 'incomer' type and urban second-homers. This state of affairs is reflected in the local property prices. The native Rockcliffeian is a virtually extinct species.

There remains abundant evidence in the area of much earlier occupation. To the south, at Castlehill Point, there was an **Iron Age fort**. Along the Jubilee Path northwards to Kippford is the prominent site of a fifth-century fortified settlement known as the **Mote of Mark**. The summit was surrounded by an earth-and-stone rampart encased in timber. Seventh-century raiders burned it down.

In its heyday, it was a sophisticated regal community with iron and bronze workshops making jewellery. Excavations have revealed glass beads and wine jars from France and glassware from Germany.

This stretch of coastline is known as the Muckle Lands and since 1937 has been in the ownership of the National Trust for Scotland. They tend it in a way designed to maximise diversity of wildlife. The butterfly population is a notable feature.

The NTS also own **Rough Island** in the firth, and run it as a bird sanctuary. The island is accessible by causeway at low-tide. Visiting during the nesting period of May and June is discouraged.

Sandyhills

The principal beach along what is sometimes, a trifle optimistically, referred to – indeed marketed as – **'The Scottish Riviera'**. Sandyhills may have its attractions, but suggesting comparison with Cannes and Nice is not helpful.

Sandyhills is disappearing – so says an official notice: 'this beach is gradually being blown away by winds, tides and human feet'. To try to keep the sand dunes intact, fences have been built as wind-breaks, and marram grass, blackthorn, brambles, broom and wild rose have been planted.

More warnings greet the visitor: about the fast-flowing incoming tide and about the deep channel offshore that is concealed by the high tide. Sandyhills has claimed lives over the years.

Senwick

Until 1618, when it was amalgamated with Borgue and Kirkandrews, Senwick was a parish in its own right. Its ancient ecclesiastical site in Senwick Wood along the west coast of Kirkcudbright Bay is one of the most charmingly secluded spots in the Stewartry.

The ruins of the old **kirk** date back to medieval times. Close by are the remains too of its manse. The buildings were abandoned in 1670. The **kirkyard**, however, continued in use for burials. It is heavily populated with dead Sproats.

When a very popular farmer called William Thomas Sproat was killed by a bull and interred here in 1923, the attendance was the biggest ever known for a funeral in the area. The cortege was over a mile long. The long, slow carrying of the coffin across the fields to the kirkyard was done by relays of farm workers. John Mactaggart, author of *The Scottish Gallovidian Encyclopedia* (see Borgue) is also buried here; his mother was a Sproat.

Just off the coast here, Kirkcudbright Bay has a feature, visible at low tide, called **Frenchman's Rock** (actually it's a group of rocks). It is said that many centuries ago, when the kirk was still in use, a party of French pirates came ashore and stole the silver, but their departure was a disaster - divine punishment, the locals thought. 'Heaven, as if jealously watching over the sacred possessions of the church, so stirred up the winds and the waves that before the robbers had succeeded in getting far from land their ship was a wreck and their earthly pilgrimage was over' (from Rev J B Henderson's history of Borgue parish, 1898).

South of Senwick kirkyard, **Balmangan** farmhouse sits next to the remains of a sixteenth-century tower-house. **Ross Bay**, which it overlooks, and its westerly neighbour **Brighouse Bay** both have evidence of their former use as harbours. Until the 1930s there was hardly an inlet along the Stewartry coast that did not have facilities for sea transport (see Part 2 - The Land and the Sea).

Senwick House, a much expanded laird's dwelling begun around 1800, was home during the 1970s to the Stewartry's pre-David Coulthard star on the racing-car circuit, **Innes Ireland** (1930-93). Innes spent his early years in Yorkshire, but his parents, who were Scottish, brought him to the Stewartry at the beginning of the Second World War. He attended Kirkcudbright Academy. His working life began as an apprentice with Rolls-Royce in Glasgow. After National Service in Egypt during the Suez Crisis of 1953-54, he took up motor racing. His first Formula One race was the Dutch Grand Prix in 1959, and in the USA, in 1961, he was the first Scot ever to win a Grand Prix. But he was sacked by Lotus and re-placed by fellow Scot Jim Clark. Returning to the Stewartry, Innes tried making a living from trawlers but it was not a great success. The remainder of his career was spent largely in journalism. His autobiography, *All Arms and Elbows*, was published in 1967. He died of cancer.

Innes Ireland

Shawhead

North-west of Shawhead are the **Glenkiln Sculptures**, a collection of works by Auguste Rodin, Jacob Epstein and Henry Moore distributed around the bleak moorland of the Glenkiln estate: a rich man's private sculpture-park that is nonetheless entirely accessible to the public. Assembling the collection began in the early 1950s - long before sculpture-parks became fashionable.

The collection was the creation of Sir William (Tony) Keswick, who was given the 3000-acre Glenkiln estate as a twenty-first birthday present in 1924. The Keswicks were the family behind the vast Hong Kong trading company Jardine Matheson.

Keswick's first acquisition was Henry Moore's *Standing Figure*. The purchase took place in the most peculiar of circumstances around 1950. Keswick had never heard of Henry Moore the sculptor. He had heard of someone called Moore who worked in metal and called at the man's workplace in search of brass bath-taps. Keswick was embarrassed to discover that this Mr Moore was unlikely to be able to provide him with bathroom accessories. But he saw *Standing Figure* – and bought it there and then. When it was delivered to Glenkiln, Keswick was away and the crate was opened by Maxie the gamekeeper, who took it to be a spare part for a tractor. Maxie always referred to it, disapprovingly, as 'Yon figure'. The Keswick family - and Moore himself, who became a close friend - continued to refer to it as 'Yon Figure'.

The second Moore piece for Glenkiln was *King and Queen*, installed in 1954, followed soon after by Jacob Epstein's *Visitation*. Moore and Epstein had cooled towards each other, and when Keswick told Epstein 'I've got a moor in Scotland', the response was 'Not that awful man!'

'Yon Figure'

Keswick's wife then persuaded him to acquire a Rodin – *John the Baptist*. After that the collection was completed by two more Moores – *Glenkiln Cross*, and *Two Piece Reclining Figure*. Henry Moore was pleased:

How important to me that Tony Keswick bought that

Shawhead

King and Queen

Standing Figure and placed it there without telling me until he invited me to see it. The setting is marvellous and so is that of the *King and Queen* and the *Cross*. All are perfectly placed. Seeing them has convinced me that sculpture – at any rate my sculpture – is best seen in this way and not in a museum.

The art historian Sir Kenneth (later Lord) Clark at first told Henry Moore that the Glenkiln location was a mistake – that his work would be damaged by exposure to the weather, while its only audience would be a flock of sheep. Clark later changed his mind:

> All great works of art should be approached in a spirit of pilgrimage. For this reason the supreme examples of siting Henry Moore's work are Tony Keswick's placements of four pieces on his sheep farm at Glenkiln. These placements could not have been achieved by a public body, however enlightened – only by an individual with a deep admiration for Moore's work, a creative imagination, and a large area to explore.

On the other hand, the Glenkiln forester Jock Murray said of the *Glenkiln Cross*: 'Reminds me of patching the bodywork of my car'.

Moore's *King and Queen* has now recovered from a malicious decapitation in 1995.

There are three other interesting 'objects' on the Glenkiln estate, all of them memorials: one for the writer and friend of the Keswicks, Peter Fleming (brother of James Bond creator Ian); a traditional Turkish widow's headstone, which Keswick took a fancy to during his travels – incised onto it are details of when the Keswicks were 'spliced'; and a simple block of local sandstone in commemoration of Henry Moore.

The **Glenkiln Reservoir**, enhancing the public water supply for Dumfries eight miles away, was created in the 1930s by damming the Old Water of Cluden.

The area is classic Covenanter country. Due north of Shawhead is **Skeoch Hill** where some 3000 Covenanters, deprived of the use of their churches, held open-air 'conventicles' in 1678.

> The face of nature did not seem propitious to the great gathering on Skeoch Hill. Inky clouds rolled athwart the leaden sky, threatening a deluge of rain, and fitful gusts of wind seemed to indicate the approach of a tempest. Nevertheless the elements were held in check by the God of nature, so that the solemn services of the day were conducted to a close without discomfort, though not altogether without interruption.
>
> *Hunted and Harried,* R M Ballantyne (1892)

The stones on Skeoch Hill are known as the 'Communion Stones' – they may have been used by the Covenanters as makeshift communion tables. The conclusion of the inscription on a monument erected in 1870 states: 'These Stones are significant memorials of those troublesome times, in which our Fathers, at the peril of their lives, contended for the great principles of civil and religious freedom'.

To the east of Skeoch Hill at **Hallhill**, by Cluden Water, is another martyrs' memorial. This one is for a couple of Covenanters who were hanged here. There is the original gravestone, but also a much later monument. The Rev C H Dick, in his *Highways and Byways in Galloway and Carrick* (1916), did not approve of what he saw:

> I should have liked to see the stone in its original simplicity. There may be some justification for the railing surrounding it; but what is to be said of the persons responsible for the tall monument erected on the very edge of the grave and telling of a congregation assembled here to listen to a sermon on the Covenanters, giving the name of the preacher, and referring to the collection made to defray the expense of this superfluous erection?

Shawhead is within the parish of Kirkpatrick-Irongray. The **kirk** is to the north-east, close to Hallhill. Its tranquil setting by Cluden Water is one of the finest ecclesiastical locations in the Stewartry. The kirkyard has a significant connection with the novelist Sir Walter Scott. A farmer's daughter, **Helen Walker** (c1710-91), provided the basis for one of Scott's best-known characters, Jeanie Deans in *The Heart of Midlothian* (1818).

Helen's sister Isabella was charged with infanticide. Helen could have secured her release by telling a little white lie. But her

Kirkpatrick-Irongray Kirk

moral integrity was so solid that she could not bring herself to do this. Her sister was duly convicted.

However, Helen then set about raising a petition for Isabella's pardon, and embarked on a 14-day barefooted walk to London to present it. Her efforts were successful.

When Helen was in old age, a woman who met her pieced together the story and sent it to Scott. As well as providing the florid words for the inscription, Scott also paid for the gravestone to be erected.

Helen Walker's grave

Southerness

T he name is a later refinement. The area's early history of **salt** production is reflected in its original name of Salterness or Satterness.

The village was developed in the late-eighteenth century by the land-owner **Richard Oswald** (1705-1784). Oswald was a remarkable man. A son of the manse from Caithness, he became a merchant in both Glasgow and London, and made a fortune as a contractor during the Seven Years' War and as an importer of Virginia tobacco. He added to his wealth by marrying Mary Ramsay whose father owned estates in America and the West Indies.

Oswald's involvement with America brought him into contact with Benjamin Franklin; the two became friends. Oswald was a British representative in Paris during 1782-3, helping to negotiate the peace treaty that brought an end to the American War of Independence.

Southerness Lighthouse

Oswald had begun his land-owning career in Scotland by acquiring the Auchencruive estate in Ayrshire (now the agricultural college of that name). His property portfolio advanced steadily southwards, culminating in his purchase of the Cavens estate by Kirkbean. He believed his Southerness land sat upon valuable coal deposits, and he built the village cottages as homes for miners. The coal turned out to be uneconomic, and thereafter the village developed as a bathing resort (which it remains, albeit as a specialist at the lower end of the holiday market).

Oswald befriended a neighbouring landowner, the 'improver' William Craik of Arbigland. The two must often have reflected upon the notoriety of that other famous participator in the American War of Independence - John Paul Jones, son of Craik's gardener (see Part 2 - The Pirate).

Southerness

The poet Robert Burns nursed an intense hatred for Oswald's wife Mary. He had known of her at Auchencruive: 'I spent my early years in her neighbourhood, and among her servants and tenants I know that she was detested with the most heartfelt cordiality'.

Mary died in 1788. Burns was intending to stay the night at a hostelry in Sanquhar when her funeral cortege arrived en route for Auchencruive. There was no longer room at the inn for Burns, and he had to ride through foul weather to New Cumnock. In a fit of resentment, he composed a poetic diatribe against the dead lady, dubbing her 'Keeper of Mammon's iron chest', and describing her husband as 'Plunderer of Armies!', a reference to Oswald's having grown rich from supplying battlefields.

Such was Mary Oswald's social status that she sat for the Royal portrait painter Johann Zoffany. The portrait now hangs prominently at the National Gallery in London.

Southerness Lighthouse is one of the oldest in Scotland. It was originally half its present height and served at first only as an unlit beacon, placed there in 1748-9 by the merchants of Dumfries as a guide to shipping on its way up the River Nith. Alterations were made in the 1780s, and again in 1842-3 when the railed walkway was added. It was lit from the 1790s. For financial reasons the light was discontinued in 1867, being re-activated in 1894 until its final extinguishment in 1936.

Southerness Golf Course, of championship status, was created in 1947 by Major Richard Oswald. It is well known for its profusion of wildlife. The golfer Tom Watson said of it: 'Listening to the myriads of natterjack toads talking to themselves in the still of a spring evening was something I will never forget'.

Springholm

*A*uchenreoch (from the Gaelic for 'gray or dun field') is the name that resonates here – the loch to the north and a bridge to the south carry it. It was only around 1800 that development took place. A 'planned village' was built along the new coach road. Its modern name is an exceedingly non-Gaelic laird's import. There was an inn for travellers, and a couple of **mills** powered by the Culshan Burn: the Auchenreoch corn mill, and the Newbank woollen mill. Today the mills are silent, but not the building-sites: the village looks increasingly like housing overspill for Castle Douglas and Dumfries.

A position on the old coach road was at first an advantage. Now that a peaceful highway has been turned into a high-speed Euro-route, it has become a curse, and much of Springholm's energy in recent years has gone into trying to persuade the passing traffic to slow down, while the campaign for a by-pass continues frustratingly. In 2005 even the local Member of Parliament was fined for exceeding the speed-limit.

North of the village, the **Barncailzie** estate was for a while the home of John Syme (1755-1831) whose claim to fame was his close friendship with the poet Robert Burns. They met after Syme was appointed distributor of stamps at Dumfries, a job he had to take up after a banking failure forced his father to sell the estate. Burns's first home in Dumfries was above Syme's office. It was Syme who accompanied the poet on his journeys through the Stewartry in the 1790s. After Burns's death in 1796, Syme defended the poet's reputation, contributed to the editing of his works and helped to raise funds for the Burns family (see Part 2 - The Bards).

Terregles

Now in effect a suburb of Dumfries, but historically very much part of the Stewartry. It was for centuries the power-base of the Maxwells, most notably Sir John Maxwell (about 1512-1583), alternatively known as Herries (after becoming the 4th Baron thereof). He was a close ally of Mary Queen of Scots, led her cavalry at the Battle of Langside in 1568, and protected her in the last days of her reign before she fled, disastrously, to England.

The **parish kirk** is surprising. The main part is largely of the nineteenth century. However, the rounded end is much older – 1580s - and has an intriguing origin. It looks like a continuation of the medieval pattern of nave and chancel. In fact it was built as a separate burial chapel by the Roman Catholic Maxwells. By keeping it formally apart from the kirk proper, the Maxwells were able to circumvent the then new Protestant stipulation that no bodies should be buried in a kirk.

In the late-eighteenth century the Maxwells had a mansion built - **Terregles House**. In the 1830s this was enlarged to the design of Sir Robert Smirke, a renowned Greek Revivalist who was the original architect of the British Museum in London. The house was demolished in 1964, but the stable-block, part of the Smirke scheme, survives.

The Maxwell name lives on in the **Maxwell Memorial Hall** of 1906. A couple of twee 1830s 'Tudor'-style cottages and a former school of the 1860s in a similar style are survivals from the days when Terregles was an estate village. The rest of modern Terregles is undistinguished.

Terregles Kirk

Tongland

Tongland's most conspicuous landmark is of course the massive Art Deco hydro-electric power station, a component of the huge 1930s water-power scheme that stretches from top to bottom of the county (see Part 2 - The Hydro).

Tongland hydro-electric power station

Tongland's history is deeper and more diverse than it would seem as you drive through. The most interesting parts of the village cannot be seen from the busy main road. Its earliest importance was as the site of an **abbey**, founded in 1218 for the Premonstratensian Order by Alan, Lord of Galloway. It was a 'daughter' house of the Order's abbey at Cockersand in Cumbria.

In the early-sixteenth century the last abbot of Tongland was an Italian fantasist called John Damian who seems to have mesmerised King James IV. Damian persuaded the king to finance his fruitless experiments in alchemy.

Damian has a special place in the ridicule of posterity as the preposterous 'Bird Man of Stirling'. He was convinced he could fly, and in 1507, wearing wings made from chicken feathers, he took off from the ramparts of Stirling Castle. His stated destination was France, but he got no further than a dunghill at the foot of the castle and broke a leg. Despite his failure, he remained a favourite of the king, who gave him a pension when he retired from Tongland in 1509. The court poet William Dunbar mercilessly mocked the mad abbot in a poem called *The Fenyeit Freir of Tungland.*

Tongland

Fragment of the abbey in the
ruin of the old parish kirk

The decaying parish kirk of 1813

A single fragment of the thirteenth-century abbey, a doorway, was incorporated into the old **parish kirk** of 1723, now a ruin. Also rapidly becoming ruinous is the replacement parish kirk of 1813.

The kirkyard contains the mausoleum of the Neilsons of Queenshill (see Ringford).

Upstream from the present power station is Tongland **Old Bridge**, completed in 1737. However, there had been previous bridges. According to some accounts, on her fateful flight from defeat at the Battle of Langside in 1568, Mary Queen of Scots crossed a wooden bridge here, which her entourage then destroyed to deter pursuit by her enemies.

The 'new' **Tongland Bridge** – downstream from the power station - was built between 1804 and 1808, to the design of the famous civil engineer Thomas Telford. The initial phase of building was a catastrophe. The foundations were washed away, and new contractors had to start again. The bridge's design is remarkable in two ways: for its appearance and for its innovatory technique. Its

The 'new' Tongland Bridge

picturesque castellated style arose from Telford commissioning the landscape artist Alexander Nasmyth to embellish his basic design. Telford's own major input was to streamline bridge construction: for the first time he substituted weight-saving hollow-ribbing for solid masonry within the structure.

There is an extraordinary story behind the factory known as the **Tongland Works** on the east bank of the river. It opened in 1917 as a subsidiary of Arrol-Johnston at Heathhall in Dumfries. Its purpose was to manufacture aero-engines for the war effort. With so many men required for front-line combat, the workforce was almost entirely female. The managing director T C Pullinger, under the influence of his visionary daughter Dorothee, treated the enterprise as an 'experiment' in making engineering attractive to women as a profession. Girls were offered three-year apprenticeships, at least two years shorter than a male one, because women, according to Pullinger, 'are born mechanics, who work with their brains as well as their hands, and they learn with astonishing rapidity. I am convinced that there is an immense future in engineering for women who really love their work and are keen on it'.

There was a great deal of interest in the factory from feminists. One who came to work here was the formidable Vera Holme, who had been active in the suffragette movement and had served as Emmeline Pankhurst's chauffeuse. She settled in Kirkcudbright for a while and was prominent in the town's artistic circles.

The design of the factory was progressive. It was based on the early automobile plants of Detroit. The walls were almost entirely of glass, reducing the need for artificial lighting. The factory had its own hydro-electric plant, which substantially reduced its energy costs. There was an emphasis on workers' amenities: a swimming-pool, a piano in the rest-room, and tennis courts on the flat roof.

At the end of the war the Tongland factory switched to the manufacture of cars, in particular a light model called The Galloway, which was described in the trade press as 'a car made by ladies for others of their sex'.

However, a trade slump of 1921 proved fatal to the factory. It closed in 1922. Later in the 1920s the factory was used by an ill-fated enterprise making artificial silk. Subsequently, the Tongland Works became a giant hen-house. Nowadays it is in a sad state of repair but still used for various commercial purposes.

Twynholm

For the 1965 *Statistical Account of Scotland*, the Rev John Good, Twynholm's minister from 1940 until 1977, wrote:

> A Scots word best describes the typical parishioner – 'bien'. The people are warm-hearted, generous and neighbourly. There is still a sense of belonging in the parish, in their outlook, and the parish is still their unit.

The community spirit of Twynholm remains strong in the twenty-first century. To mark the start of a new millennium, a village committee published an impressive history, and a new community garden was created for the same purpose.

The orientation of Twynholm is pleasingly simple. On top is Main Street (blessedly relieved of A75 traffic by the building of a by-pass in the 1970s). Then there are three braes – Burn Brae, Kirk Brae and Captain's Brae (formerly Parish Brae but re-named after a captain who lived there), all meeting in the hollow of the 'holm' through which runs a burn.

At the intersection of the braes is a former woollen mill which continued to operate until the late 1920s. Its products included blankets, an example of which is held by the Stewartry Museum in Kirkcudbright.

The present **kirk** is of 1818, with major renovations in 1913-14 and a porch added in 1954 ('...the days of brides being blown to pieces or drooked on the doorstep have gone...').

The kirkyard is much older. It has a poignant memorial to an entire family of seven – parents and five children - who were wiped out in 1816 by the collapse of a gravel pit, where they had been spending the night during a journey across Galloway. On the original gravestone the anonymous father is described as a Welsh soldier. Years later more information about him was dis-

Twynholm Kirk

covered, and in 1946 a second gravestone was erected by the Galloway Association of Glasgow. On this he is named not only as Hugh Prichard but also as the original 'minstrel' on whom Sir Walter Scott based 'Wandering Willie' in *Redgauntlet* (1824).

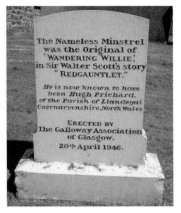

Also buried here is Andrew McRobert, one of five Covenanters killed in 1685 by Grierson of Lag and his men on Kirkconnel Moor (see Ringford).

In recent years Twynholm has gained international recognition as the birthplace of Formula One racing-driver **David Coulthard** (born 1971). The David Coulthard Museum opened in 1999, followed in 2000 by an adjoining café called The Pit Stop Diner.

Before David's time, however, the Coulthard name was already widely disseminated. The livery of the lorries operated by the family haulage firm Hayton Coulthard has long been familiar up and down the motorways of the UK.

David's great-grandfather established the Twynholm dynasty. Peter Coulthard came here from Penrith at the beginning of the twentieth century. He worked initially as a tailor. The haulage business began in 1916 when he invested in a motor-bike and side-car for the distribution of newspapers. With his first lorry he collected milk-cans from farms for delivery to the creamery. At his first depot (where the village garage now is) there was a disastrous fire in 1927. The business was in ruins until the villagers held a whist-drive and raised £40 to help him get started again.

As the business expanded, Peter set up a depot in the building that would later house his great-grandson's museum. The business passed into the hands of Peter's son Jimmy, then Jimmy's widow Margaret, followed by their son Duncan (David's father), who was succeeded by Duncan Jnr.

David Coulthard

141

Twynholm

The **Star Hotel** on Main Street was established at the beginning of the twentieth century by a Dalbeattie businessman who named it after Dalbeattie Star football team. Its name has inspired a raft of local jokes revolving around a local who, on having the Star of Bethlehem pointed out to him, replied 'But I wish it was the Star o Twynholm'. Before the liberalisation of Scotland's drinking laws, the Star was a favourite Sabbath destination for Kirkcudbright's more enthusiastic tipplers, who walked the three miles to Twynholm in order to qualify and be served as 'bona fide' travellers.

South-east of the village, at the confluence of the Tarff and Dee rivers, sprawls the **Cumstoun** estate. The house, in Tudor-Gothic style, is of 1828, with later additions of the 1890s. Beside it are the ruins of a fifteenth-century castle. It was here that the late-sixteenth-century poet Alexander Montgomerie is reputed to have composed his best-known work, *The Cherrie and the Slae,* in which – at considerable length – he debates whether he should reach out for the cherry on the cliff or content himself with the more accessible sloe.

Cumstoun came into the ownership of the Maitland family at the beginning of the nineteenth century. The most distinguished of the line was Thomas Maitland (1792-1851), a lawyer with literary interests who took the title of Lord Dundrennan when he became a Court of Session judge. Before that he had been Solicitor-General for Scotland and MP for the Stewartry of Kirkcudbright.

Barwhinnock, an early-nineteenth-century, whinstone-built private house to the north-west of Twynholm, invariably attracts the admiring attention of architectural historians passing through the county. One rates it as 'classy' and 'deliciously smart'. Another describes it as '*soigné*' and its interior as 'a stunner' ('...double-height hall with paired stairs ascending in horseshoe curve to fluted Doric-screened landing...'). The house was built for Major James Irving of the Bengal Cavalry.

Part Two

THEMES
and
PERSONALITIES

The Early History

When the story of these parts begins, there is no Stewartry, nor even the wider region of Galloway. The earliest times here – beginning with the first human presence possibly around 6000 BC - were much like those in any other part of the British Isles: the long, slow evolution of civilisation from the Stone Age through the Bronze Age to the Iron Age. The reader's patience need not be taxed with a repetition of the textbook generalities with which we are all familiar from our schooldays.

We shall jump several millennia, therefore, and take up the story at the point where it starts to be exciting. The year is 82 AD, and, much to the surprise and alarm of the Britonnic tribes, the Romans have arrived.

The Romans

The Romans had been well entrenched in the south of what they called Britannia for some forty years before they turned their attention to the inhabitants of Caledonia. It was only after a thorough reconnaissance of the Picts of the far north that they finally came to the South-West under the command of Julius Agricola.

'Novantae' was the name they gave to the people they found along the Solway. The local tribes were by no means ignorant and unskilled savages. They had a sophistication of their own in their hill-forts and their crannogs, those ingenious defensible homes built upon wooden piles driven into the bed of a loch, a building technique they were employing long before the Venetians had a similar idea. They also traded extensively.

Modern reconstruction of a crannog

Life in a crannog

The marching-camps the Romans established in the area – a substantial one at Glenlochar on the River Dee and a smaller presence up the valley from Gatehouse of Fleet – were not known about until the 1940s when the settlements were revealed by new techniques of aerial archaeology. It is likely that the Romans explored as far west as the Wigtownshire coast, contemplating but never finally attempting an invasion of Ireland.

The Novantae were never a serious threat to the Romans. During the four centuries of their hold over Britannia, the Romans' interest in the northern Solway area was only intermittent. Their Glenlochar base was abandoned and dismantled at one point, and later re-built.

When, after about 140 AD, the Romans more or less retreated behind Hadrian's Wall, the South-West was simply an area to keep half an eye on. They and the locals accommodated each other. A kind of *pax romana* pertained until, finally, with their over-extended empire starting to unravel, the Romans abandoned Britannia around 410 AD.

Christianity

The Romans, who officially adopted Christianity in 312, may well have helped spread the gospel before they left these shores. The South-West is commonly described as having been Scotland's 'cradle of Christianity': Bishop Ninian is said to have begun his mission from Whithorn a generation before Columba began his from Iona.

Early History

According to the traditional account (unreliably based on chronicles composed centuries later), Ninian was the son of a local chieftain who travelled to Rome for priestly training. He is said to have returned home in 397, founding his 'Candida Casa' church at Whithorn and setting off on a mission to convert the pagan Picts.

Among modern scholars, however, there is no consensus about who this man was - if he existed - and when he operated. Some interpretations of the flimsy evidence have him active in the sixth rather than the fifth century. It has even been suggested that there may have been *two* Ninians, one for each century.

Whatever the truth may be, it seems certain that Whithorn was a Christian settlement from at least the fifth century, and the idea of the saintly Ninian took such a hold over the Christian imagination that for many centuries pilgrims made their way across the South-West to pray at his Whithorn shrine. King Robert I, the victor of Bannockburn, visited during his final illness, and King James IV was a regular supplicant until his death in 1513.

More Invasions

After the Romans departed, the South-West was subjected to wave after wave of invasion and immigration from all directions. First it became part of the kingdom of Rheged, whose centre of power was in modern Cumbria. Then the Angles arrived, having migrated to the east coast of England from their Germanic homeland and spread steadily westwards. The Anglian culture was sufficiently embedded by the eighth century for Whithorn to have become an Anglian bishopric, although the original Brittonic society had not been entirely eliminated.

The ethnic mix got more complex with periodic influxes of people from Ireland and from Scandinavia. The Irish were the aboriginal Scots whose eventual settlement in Argyll – their kingdom of Dalriada - would later form the basis for the creation of modern Scotland.

The whole of the western seaboard as far north as the Hebrides was being targeted by these Scots and by the Vikings, and over time the two ethnic groups seem to have intermingled in a kind of Hiberno-Norse genetic whirlpool. From this mix there apparently arose a hybrid people described as Gall Gaidhil, meaning either *stranger Gael* or *Scandinavian Gael*. By the tenth century they had a substantial presence in the South-West, and the traditional theory is that their name evolved into the geographical term Galloway. It has to be said, however, that that theory is now being disputed by some more recent historians.

The ethnic diversity of the South-West through the Dark Ages also brought an extraordinary linguistic complexity. The Britonnic tribes spoke Cumbric, a Celtic tongue that survives in modern Welsh; the Angles introduced an early form of Old English; the Irish Scots were Gaelic speakers; and the Scandinavians had their own Norse language. From all of these linguistic options, it was Gaelic that eventually became dominant, only much later being replaced by Scots and English (see The Language).

By the eleventh century Galloway had finally and indisputably come into existence as a separate state with not only a common language but also an aristocratic dynasty to rule over it.

The Lordship of Galloway

The separate realm of Galloway had clearly been in the hands of a ruling aristocracy for some time, but we don't know who exactly they were - until one of them suddenly appears on the scene in the early 1100s, a fully recognisable character to whom at last we can give a name. Welcome to **Fergus**, Lord of Galloway, or, as he preferred to put it, *rex Galwitensium*, king of the Gallovidians. He and his descendents continued to rule a more or less independent territory for the next two hundred years.

Fergus's Galloway was in a pivotal position in the diplomatic manoeuvrings of the Irish Sea zone. To the north was a still evolving Scotland; to the south, England; and, in the middle of the Irish Sea, the kingdom of Man. All three had reason to woo Fergus and he was adept at playing one off another. With a ready supply of fighting-men whose mercenary services were often sought after, little Galloway had the ability to punch above its weight.

Fergus strengthened his position through a series of politically shrewd marital ties. He himself was married to an illegitimate daughter of Henry I of England. His own daughter Affreca married the king of Man, while one of his sons, Uchtred, was hitched to a relative of David I of Scotland. This range of connections served as a ring of defence around the independence of Galloway.

Nevertheless, Fergus had a problem, and it was within his own family. His two sons, **Uchtred** and **Gilbert**, were venomously jealous of one another, each believing that he had a stronger claim to be their father's heir. Both were restless and ambitious, and agitated for action against the Scots.

Perhaps to placate them at the same time as reasserting his authority over them, Fergus took the opportunity of King Malcolm IV's absence abroad to launch a raid on Scottish territory. It was a big mistake. When Malcolm arrived home, the Scots invaded to teach the Gallovidians a lesson.

Early History

Fergus made peace by ignominiously abdicating, spending the final year of his life as a penitent at the abbey of Holyrood in Edinburgh. King Malcolm was now able to dictate the way forward in Galloway, and he went for a policy of 'divide and rule' by splitting the province into two: Gilbert got western Galloway, while Uchtred was apportioned the eastern half. The kingdom of the Scots had moved a step closer to its ultimate goal of assimilating its smaller southern neighbour.

Yet the two sons of Fergus continued to feud. In 1174 Gilbert murdered Uchtred, but he was denied the prize of a re-united Galloway. With Scottish help, Uchtred's son Roland gained control of the east and, when Gilbert died in 1185, of the whole.

Until his own death in 1200, **Roland** maintained at least a partial independence for Galloway while at the same time moving closer to the Scottish king, adopting the Scottish policy of encouraging Anglo-Norman immigration which his grandfather Fergus had firmly resisted. He led a kind of double life, a semi-detached magnate in his own right who yet held office within the Scottish royal household. In 1200 he was with William I of Scotland on a diplomatic mission to King John of England. But while down south he died and was buried in Northampton.

Roland's son **Alan** took over as Lord of Galloway. He too had good dynastic connections throughout the British Isles, his second wife, Margaret, being a niece of the Scottish King and all his daughters being married off to significant Anglo-Norman barons. He was courted for his military capability, which included a substantial navy. At times it was expedient for him to throw his weight behind the Scottish king; at other times he did military favours for King John of England. In 1215 he was by the side of King John at Runnymede for the signing of the Magna Carta.

Alan's career was overshadowed, however, by concern for his succession. He had plenty of healthy daughters, but all his legitimate sons died young. After his second wife's death, he contracted yet another marriage in a desperate attempt to produce another son. But he died before this could be accomplished.

Among the fighting men of Galloway, who were keen to maintain its independence, there was a spurt of support for Alan's illegitimate son Thomas as the heir. Exploiting what they believed to be their overlordship, the Scots intervened. Thomas was captured and imprisoned. From then on Galloway was effectively a part of Scotland.

Alan's extensive land-holdings were intact, however, and they were divided amongst his daughters. Eventually, through the death of her siblings, the youngest daughter, **Dervorguilla,** inherited the entire portfolio and styled herself Lady of Galloway, though there was no longer the political power to go with the prestige. There were more inheritances from her mother's side of the family, and further accretions of land through marrying John de Balliol, an Anglo-Norman nobleman from northern England, whose family retained their original estates in Picardy. With their combined resources across three countries, Dervorguilla and John de Balliol were one of the golden couples of western Europe in the thirteenth century.

After John's death in 1268/9, Dervorguilla lavished much of her wealth on two vast projects in his memory: the building of Sweetheart Abbey (see Part 1 - New Abbey), and the founding of Balliol College, Oxford, whose charter she signed in 1282 at Buittle Castle in the Urr Valley.

Dervorguilla outlived all of her eight children except one, her youngest son John. No one could realistically have foreseen what would happen to him. What did happen means that there is one final attribute to be added to the profile of this extraordinary woman: mother of a monarch.

Dervorguilla's Son Becomes King

Towards the end of the thirteenth century Kirkcudbrightshire became central to the question of who would rule Scotland. Through the royal bloodline descending from Dervorguilla's mother, her son John became one of two principal claimants to the, unexpectedly vacant, throne.

In 1286 King Alexander III fell from his horse and died, leaving no children. The next-in-line was his infant grand-daughter Margaret, 'The Maid of Norway'. Six guardians were appointed until she came of age, but in 1290 she too died. It was now a choice between John de Balliol of Buittle and Robert de Brus (grandfather of the more famous Bruce of Bannockburn).

And who was asked by the nobles to make the choice? None other than King Edward I of England, who welcomed every opportunity to meddle in Scottish affairs. He agreed to adjudicate on condition that whoever was crowned would acknowledge the English monarch as overlord. Not surprisingly, Edward opted for the weaker of the two candidates, John de Balliol. The man from Buittle was duly crowned in 1292. But he was never more than his nickname suggests – 'Toom Tabard', empty coat.

Balliol's one show of strength brought English retribution. In 1296 Edward and his army entered Scotland and Balliol surrendered his throne. The strongholds of the Stewartry, including the Balliol castle at Buittle, fell into English hands, and in 1300 Edward himself returned and embarked on a grand military procession through the Stewartry, his army encamping at Kirkcudbright, Twynholm, Enrick near Gatehouse of Fleet, Crossmichael and New Abbey.

War of Independence

Edward and his army returned to Dumfries where they strengthened the castle and made it the headquarters for their rule over the South-West. Meanwhile, **Robert Bruce**, grandson of one of the earlier claimants, having murdered his nearest rival, set about terrorising the occupying English, and made enough progress to get himself crowned King of Scotland.

The war of attrition continued. For a time Bruce's life was in such danger that he took to the Stewartry hills around Loch Trool. It was there that Bruce and his men scored one of their more daring victories. While Bruce widened his theatre of operations to the rest of Scotland, his brother **Edward Bruce** was left in charge of the South-West with the title of Lord of Galloway.

Once Robert had secured freedom for Scotland through the Battle of Bannockburn in 1314, Kirkcudbrightshire did not see him again, apart from one visit in 1329 towards the end of his life.

Another Balliol in the Hot Seat

In 1329 the new king, David II, was just five years old. His minority was another opportunity for the English king, this time Edward III, to manoeuvre his way back into Scottish affairs. **Edward Balliol**, son of 'Toom Tabard', was installed as King of Scotland, but he was nothing more than an puppet of the English. Balliol took up residence in the old family seat of Buittle, the only place in Scotland where he felt relatively safe. Eventually, the Scots won back the South-West, David II came of age, and the English were never again in control of Kirkcudbrightshire.

Beginnings of the Stewartry

Now the stage in the story at which the term Stewartry originates. King David placed the administration of the South-West in the hands of the Douglases. In 1369 Archibald ('The Grim') Douglas was created Lord of Galloway and put in charge of the lands between the Nith and the Cree that form modern Kirkcudbrightshire.

Being a man with interests elsewhere in Scotland, Archibald appointed a 'steward' to act on his behalf, and so 'The Stewartry' was born. Archibald built Threave Castle near Castle Douglas as his south-western stronghold. It was there that he died in 1400.

Subsequent Douglases got above themselves and there was continual conflict between them and the Crown until, in 1455, King James II came personally to Threave and forced the 9th Earl of Douglas into exile. Douglas had no heirs and all other senior members of his clan had died, mainly fighting. When he himself died in 1488 the 'Black Douglas' dynasty of Threave was no more.

The Reformation

The sixteenth and seventeenth centuries in the Stewartry, as else-where in Scotland, were marred by conflicts over religion. The new Presbyterianism of the Reformation under the leadership of John Knox was established in 1560. But **Mary Queen of Scots** re-mained Roman Catholic. When her Protestant opponents de-feated her in 1568 at the Battle of Langside, she fled to the Stew-artry, under the protection of Lord Herries of Terregles: the South-West, despite Presbyterianism having taken root, retained a cer-tain loyalty to the monarchy. It was here that she last stood on Scottish soil before embarking on her ultimately fatal journey to the England of her cousin Elizabeth I (see Part 1 - Dundrennan).

Mary was succeeded by her son who became **James VI**. While broadly accepting Presbyterianism, he refused to abolish the office of bishop – and thus were sown the seeds of further religious con-flict in the following century, with appalling consequences for the life of the Stewartry.

The Covenanters

For more than half of the seventeenth century Scotland was riven by bitter and violent religious controversy, and nowhere in the land was the great struggle between Presbyteries and Prelates more passionately joined than in the Stewartry.

After the Union of the Crowns in 1603, King James, now 1st of England as well as 6th of Scotland, transferred his court to London. He had already demonstrated his dislike of the puritanical Calvin-ists of his homeland, and this deepened in exile into a southern contempt.

James dearly wished to cement the Union of the two countries and chose to do so by promoting uniformity of worship, which in practice meant the imposition upon Scotland of English ecclesias-tical structures of a kind redolent to the Scots of the dreaded 'Popery'. James's son, Charles I, was even more insensitive in his handling of the matter, and in 1638 revulsion for the English prayer-book and rule by bishops led to the mass signing by Scot-tish Presbyterians of the National Covenant in support of 'the true religion'. But even the beheading of King Charles in 1649 did not bring freedom of worship for the Covenanters, nor did the Solemn League and Covenant of 1643, their military pact with the anti-monarchists during the Civil War. The Cromwell regime simply reneged on their promises.

With the Restoration of 1660, the situation got no better. Charles II was as insistent as his predecessors had been on turning the Church of Scotland into the Church of England. Ministers were ousted from their posts in favour of poorly trained yes-men, and the congregations took to the hills to worship at open-air 'conventicles'.

King and Covenanters went to war. The animosity was intensified by the unyielding nastiness of the leadership on both sides. The Covenanters were by now dominated by the extremists, fanatics reminiscent of the suicide-bombers of the twenty-first century. In the rogues' gallery of Crown-appointed sadists who masterminded the repression in the Stewartry, two names stand out: Sir John Graham of Claverhouse and Sir Robert Grierson of Lag.

The bloodshed culminated in 'The Killing Times' of 1684-86 during which at least 82 Galloway people were summarily executed. The moors and hillsides of the Stewartry abound in memorials to what are always referred to as 'martyrs'. There is hardly a kirkyard in the county without at least one Covenanter gravestone.

Freedom of worship was finally secured only with the Revolution Settlement of 1690, when Protestant William and Mary were invited to replace Catholic James VII and II.

The Zealots

Now back in the ascendancy, Stewartry Presbyterianism fell under the influence of zealots who revelled in putting the fear of God into the people. Even innocent pleasures were condemned as debauchery. Dancing, in particular, was frowned upon as an incentive to sensuality – 'an inlet to lust and provocation to uncleanness'. Pre-marital sexual relations were punished by humiliation in front of the congregation. Hard-working people, whose lives were likely to be relatively short and disease-ridden, continued to seek escape in drinking and fornication, though in most cases they believed the ministers and elders who told them they would roast in Hell. There were few opportunities for simple enjoyment – and the newly triumphant Kirk did its utmost to deny them even those.

The kirk leaders were merciless in their pursuit of another form of alleged deviancy, so-called 'witchcraft', which was seen as the Devil's way of undermining the kirk. The 'witches' were often just dotty old ladies behaving oddly, but they were convenient scapegoats for anything going wrong, particularly crop failure. Drowning and burning alive were common punishments.

Elspeth McEwan from the parish of Balmaclellan was the last 'witch' to be killed by the authorities. Among other things, she was accused of causing her neighbour's hens to stop laying. She endured two years' imprisonment in Kirkcudbright Tolbooth awaiting trial, during which she was tortured until she 'confessed'. The conditions were so appalling that she frequently pleaded with her jailers to end her life.

Elspeth eventually got her way. At her trial she was found guilty of a 'compact and correspondence with the Devil', and in 1698 was burned at the stake. Among the official expenses for the occasion was the sum of two shillings for 'ane pint of aill' for the executioner. Later, non-capital punishments included unlimited banishment from the area. The laws against 'witchcraft' were not repealed until 1736.

Union with England

With Presbyterianism so firmly established in the South-West, it is not surprising that the 1715 and 1745 Jacobite rebellions, aimed at restoring the exiled Catholic Stuart line to the throne, were largely ignored in the Stewartry. The involvement of William Gordon, Viscount Kenmure, who was executed in 1716 for supporting the futile cause, was not typical (see Part 1 - New Galloway).

In the years following the 1707 Union between Scotland and England, the folk of the Stewartry were more concerned about how they were going to rise out of their habitual poverty. At first the Union brought no obvious economic benefits. Worse than that: it brought new taxes on goods, so the people took with guilt-free enthusiasm to the smuggling trade. Seaboard access, natural hiding-places along the shore and a network of discreet pathways across the hills meant that the Stewartry became the hub of contraband distribution for the whole of southern Scotland (see Part 1 - Auchencairn).

The Union did open up new English markets for the Stewartry cattle trade, and the big landowners saw that that could be the way forward to a new prosperity. What it required, though, was a radical overhaul in land-use and so, throughout the eighteenth century, the crude pastureland of the Stewartry underwent an extraordinary transformation into the 'landscape of improvement' which we look out upon to this day. That is a story which will be taken up in the next chapter.

The Land and the Sea

The Stewartry is like Scotland in miniature, a compact show-case of the whole landscape experience north of the border. Every aspect popularly associated with picturesque Scotland is represented here in concentrated and accessible form: highlands and lowlands, lochs, glens, salmon rivers, rocky coast, sandy shore and mudflats. The undulating, lush-green lowland of the coastline gives way in the northern region to a moorlandish and mountainous terrain. The summits may, strictly speaking, qualify as hills rather than mountains, but they have sufficient grandeur, ruggedness and remoteness for them to be referred to as the Stewartry Highlands.

In the beginning - five, or possibly as much as six, hundred million years ago (what's the odd hundred million years between geologist friends?) - there was just sea. Then the water receded and the accumulation of sand, shale, mud, silt and pebbles dried and hardened into what is now the *sedimentary* bedrock of the Stewartry. This in turn was broken and twisted by the upward movement of molten material that petrified into the *igneous* rock of the Stewartry hills: the great granite masses of Criffel, Cairnsmore and Mullwharchar. The *metamorphic* effect of these intrusions was to ripple the bedrock into the shapes with which we are now familiar. But the sculpting of the land was not over yet. A succession of ice ages followed, the last of them taking place as relatively recently as some ten thousand years ago. Massive bodies of ice scraped and scoured the rocks and deposited detritus along the valley bottoms.

Hundreds of millions of years later, the fields to be laid out for the expanding cattle trade were cleared of the ice-age boulders and the pioneer drystane-dykers had a ready-made supply of material for their new enclosures. Meanwhile, when the builders of houses and farm steadings moved from timber to stone, the bedrock yielded *whinstone*, the county's characteristic building material, and the igneous rock provided *granite* for the sills and the lintels, while just over the border in Dumfriesshire there was fine red *sandstone* workable enough for the mason to carve into the decorative trimmings. The built environment of the Stewartry came to express, with a simplicity that is the essence of beauty, the secrets of the rocks below.

154

The Stewartry landscape of today is far from natural. Its appearance has evolved through centuries of human intervention. The patchwork of fields enclosed by drystane-dykes, the woodlands deliberately placed as shelter-belts and game nurseries, the manicured parklands of the big estates – all are elements in a classic example of 'the landscape of improvement', the legacy of an **agrarian revolution** that transformed the Stewartry from the early-eighteenth century onwards.

Before 1700 agriculture in the Stewartry had barely changed for centuries. Much of the land was boggy and barren. Primitive farming activity, throughout the sixteenth and seventeenth centuries, was clustered around ferm-touns of perhaps six to eight families. The cultivation of the land was organised on the infield-outfield pattern. The infield was the better land immediately adjacent to the settlement. This was inefficiently shared out into small parcels on the 'run-rig' system, a series of long strips divided by uncultivated borders.

Almost the only crops grown were bere (barley) for ale-making and oats for food. The outfield alternated between crops and grazing. The rest of the land was open rough pasture, unfenced and undrained. Cattle were kept largely for pulling ploughs, not for human consumption.

Towards the end of the seventeenth century the need to use land more efficiently was starting to be appreciated. In the early decades of the following century some larger landowners were emerging as 'Improvers'. After the opening up of the vast English market following the Union of the Parliaments in 1707, they saw fresh opportunities for trading. The Stewartry's outstanding example was William Craik of Arbigland (see Part 1 - Kirkbean).

It had become increasingly difficult to organise the cattle-droving trade, the mass movement of livestock southwards to the markets of England. Enclosure helped to stop roving beasts from trampling over crops and facilitated the disciplined gatherings of livestock for pre-market fattening. In the longer term, enclosure also aided the development of more successful breeding programmes. These entrepreneurial landowners also introduced new crop species, experimented with more sophisticated methods of keeping the soil fertile, and implemented schemes for draining the sodden land.

The enclosure method was **drystane dyking**. Centuries later we now appreciate this sturdy stone walling as one of the glories of the Stewartry countryside. They are stunningly clever forms of agricultural masonry, constructed entirely without mortar and capable of standing for hundreds of years. Sadly, in many cases, the modern cash-strapped farmer, faced with a gap to be repaired, resorts to cheap barbed-wire, the hostile ugliness of which is heart-breaking.

Dyking developed across most of eighteenth-century Scotland, but the pioneering principles were established in the Stewartry. The first large-scale scheme was undertaken at Palgown in the west of the county around 1710. By the time the land had been comprehensively enclosed, there were some 7000 miles of dykes, some of them on alarmingly precipitous terrain.

A typical Stewartry dyke began with a six-inch trench for the *foundations* made up of tightly packed small flat stones. If, however, a big boulder embedded into the ground was in the proposed line of the dyke, it would be ingeniously incorporated into the structure. A tapering *double* dyke with infill called *hearting* was then built on the foundations. Before it had reached the two-feet mark, flat stones large enough to cover the width of the wall plus a slight overhang formed a stabilising *through band*. Another tapering double dyke with hearting continued upwards, and this was topped by another through band called the *cover band*. The dyke was then finished off with a row of *cope stones*.

The final height was usually at least four and a half feet but could be anything up to six feet. A common variation is known as the *Galloway Hedge*: a dyke combined with a hedge of thorns planted to grow through the lower wall and then up the other side.

At first the new dykes provoked a furious reaction. Many of the

Section through a typical Stewartry dyke

A drystane dyking competition

country workers were upset by the loss of common grazing, tenant farmers were angered by notices to quit, and in 1723 the discontent suddenly erupted into a movement known as **The Levellers**. They swept across the county, 'levelling' dykes wherever they found them. They were so effective at this that government troops were called in. Various truces were agreed, only to be followed by more outbursts in 1724.

A final confrontation took place at Duchrae in the parish of Balmaghie. The Levellers were heavily defeated by the troops. Many were arrested, but the humaneness of the commanding officer enabled a large number of them to escape, and at subsequent trials the ringleaders were fined rather than hanged. Some of the landowners complained about this apparent leniency, to which the commanding officer gave this remarkably liberal response:

> When I was sent here in command of the troops, my instructions were to suppress rebellious mobs, instead of which I find an oppressed, persecuted, suffering people, committing some irregularities; and I think it below the dignity of his majesty's field officers to act severely to such a people.

Nowadays dyking is regarded as a venerable tradition. Competitions are held regularly and the old art is enjoying something of a revival.

The Land and the Sea

Part of the Corse of Slakes road

At the same time as the land was being improved and enclosed, the Stewartry's primitive **road system** (drove-roads, pack-ways, smugglers' trails and pilgrims' routes) was also receiving attention.

The government in London was keen to improve land communication between England and Ireland for the movement of troops. In 1763-4 a major west-east highway was built. It can still be seen, here and there, on maps as the Old Military Road. Over much of the route, the military engineers simply upgraded existing pathways: widening, straightening and re-surfacing. There were some brand-new stretches, like the spectacular Corse of Slakes section between Creetown and Anwoth, which one historian has described enthusiastically as 'perhaps the most fascinating length of military road outwith the Highlands, with a remarkable hair-pin bend on Ardwall Hill and a number of interesting old bridges'.

More new Kirkcudbrightshire roads followed: Rhonehouse to Twynholm via Tongland and Tarff (1768-72); Dalbeattie north to Kirkpatrick Durham (1772-7); and the coastal route between Gatehouse and Creetown (1786-90). But land communications around the Stewartry still left much to be desired. The roads were described by an observer in 1792 as 'universally miry and unsolid'.

For improvement to be sustained new sources of finance were required and the county turned to the idea of turnpike trusts which raised the necessary capital through toll-charging. Numerous significant highways were laid by this method through the first half of the nineteenth century, with mighty new bridges over the Cree in the west, the Ken at New Galloway and the Dee at Threave.

Viewed from the land, the Stewartry has always been, and to some extent remains, relatively remote from the main concentrations of population. But look at it from the **sea** and at once it becomes obvious why the Stewartry was for a long time in its history at the heart of a great maritime region.

In the twelfth and thirteenth centuries the Lords of Galloway, big players in the dynastic politics of the Irish Sea and Celtic western seaboard, could muster a sizeable navy (see The Early History). From early-medieval times until the closing decades of the nineteenth century, commercial traffic in and out of the Stewartry ports was astonishingly extensive. Ships took away grain, potatoes, turnips, sheep and cattle and returned with whatever could not be produced locally. They went to Liverpool and Glasgow for manufactured goods, to Brittany for wine, to the West Indies for sugar, rum and tobacco, and to Canada and the Baltic for hardwoods. The ships transported people too, whether emigrants or trippers. What is now a long and circuitous journey by land to, for example, Whitehaven in Cumberland was by sea a straightforward affair from port to port across the Solway Firth. Journeys by sea southwards to the port of Liverpool, across to Ireland and the Isle of Man and up the west coast to the Clyde and beyond were all routine. To the sailor of the eighteenth and nineteenth centuries, the Stewartry must have seemed like the centre of the universe!

There were, as a result, many more harbours along the Stewartry coast than is immediately apparent today. Communities that now seem almost land-locked have, on closer inspection, surprising vestiges of a seafaring tradition.

In the west of the county, bordering Wigtown Bay, tiny Palnure had a creek serving the nearby lead-mines; Creetown, though now severed from the sea by the A75 by-pass, had a modest harbour in its centre; and the granite quarries at Kirkmabreck and Carsluith had their dedicated quays for export, mainly to Liverpool. At Gatehouse of Fleet there was Port McAdam, made possible when the river's upper reach was canalised in the 1820s. Towards the east of the county, the River Urr was navigable up to Palnackie by 350-ton vessels and, unlikely as it may seem nowadays, smaller ships could get as far upstream as Dalbeattie. Kippford was not always the leisure port it is today – it had shipbuilding yards. Still further east, Carsethorn operated as a port for Dumfries, with a regular steam-packet service to and from Liverpool. Today, of all these, only the harbour at Kirkcudbright remains significant commercially.

From the middle of the nineteenth century, the county's shipping companies had a new rival: the **railway** had arrived. As a result, by the end of the century, the harbours of the Stewartry were becoming moribund. The first section of the railway to be opened, in 1859, was the Dumfries to Castle Douglas line. 1861 saw the completion of the Portpatrick Railway, linking Castle Douglas with the west coast ferry terminal. A branch-line from Castle Douglas to Kirkcudbright followed in 1864. As each section opened, there were great celebrations. Creetown, for example, had a 'grand ball' to welcome its new station.

A Stewartry station in the age of steam

The chosen route across the Stewartry was seemingly bizarre, and certainly controversial at the time. Instead of following the fairly level coastline, the promoters opted for a route through remote hill and moor country. This option, although requiring much excavation and the building of great viaducts, was more direct and therefore cheaper to build. From Castle Douglas the line went north up the Ken-Dee valley via Crossmichael. At Parton it turned west across a handsome metal bridge over the Ken/Dee and into a virtually unpopulated wilderness until descending back down to the coast at Creetown.

The people of Gatehouse of Fleet were furious at being ignored in the proposed route and demanded to see the engineers' survey, but it was kept secret. At last a concession was made to them - they could have a station but it would be some six miles to the north of the town along the moorland stretch between Loch Skerrow and Creetown. The railway company had to pay for a new road link between the station and the town.

This compromise halt underwent an extraordinary series of name changes. When it opened in 1861 it was Dromore. In 1863 it was switched to Gatehouse. Two years later it had become Dromore for Gatehouse, though the following year it reverted back to Gatehouse. In 1871 it was once again Dromore. Finally, in 1912, it settled as Gatehouse of Fleet.

Some considered the route eccentric, but the result was one of the most dramatically scenic railway lines in the British Isles – the setting of Richard Hannay's escape in *The Thirty-Nine Steps*, and forever a favourite with devotees of railway romance.

Just for the record, the journey from the Cree in the west to the Nith in the east had the following stations: Newton Stewart, Pal-

A steam train crossing the Loch Ken Viaduct near Parton

nure, Creetown, Gatehouse of Fleet, Loch Skerrow Halt, New Galloway (Mossdale), Parton, Crossmichael, Castle Douglas, Buittle (briefly), Dalbeattie, Southwick, Kirkgunzeon, Killywhan (Beeswing), Lochanhead, Maxwelltown and Dumfries. The branch-line from Castle Douglas to Kirkcudbright had stops at Bridge of Dee (until 1949) and at Tarff.

In 1963 there was a spectacular accident at Kirkcudbright station – fortunately without any serious injury. The brakes on a goods train failed on the descent from Tarff, and a carriage passed through the buffers and ended up in the wall of a sweetie-shop on the opposite side of Bridge Street.

In 1965 the whole of the Stewartry's railway system was brought to a halt. It had been felled by a radical review of the railways that came to be known, after its author, as 'The Beeching Axe'. The great viaducts remain, as do tantalising stretches of disused line – all painful reminders of what the Stewartry might still have had if the concept of 'greenness' had taken hold several decades earlier.

Train crash in Kirkcudbright

Belted Galloway calf

The arrival of the railway in the middle of the nineteenth century had a huge impact on Stewartry agriculture. Until then the rearing of livestock had been mainly for **beef** production. The ancient Galloway breed, with its thick black coat against the harshness of winter, became world-famous, as did the strikingly different Belted Galloway which has served so well as an iconic image for the county. But now cattle farmers were diversifying into **dairying** to meet the growing demand for milk and its by-products for the often malnourished workers of Scotland's industrial belt. Transport by rail could get the milk to Glasgow and the towns of Lanarkshire before it went sour.

It was the Stewartry's northern neighbour Ayrshire that first developed a dairy breed with a particularly high yield. Initially, the farmers of the Stewartry resisted the Ayrshire cows, but eventually they became the staple breed, augmented in more recent times by the Friesian and the Holstein.

Dairying was a highly labour-intensive activity. Ways were continually being sought to mechanise it. A breakthrough came in the 1890s when Stewart Nicholson (1865-1956) of Bombie farm near Kirkcudbright began experimenting with the idea of a **milking machine**. His inspiration was strife among the milkmaids:

> I have seen many a can of milk thrown during a fracas. It meant I had to be in the byre at 5.00 am and 5.00 pm to keep the peace. I began thinking this was an awful tie when I should be doing something else and wondering if there was no other means of getting the milking done...one day the idea came into my head – copy the suckling calf – just like that!

Nicholson's invention – with teat connectors made of horn and rubber – proved to be not quite the right thing, and at the Wallace foundry in Castle Douglas the experimentation continued. Milking by machine did not come into common usage until after the Second World War. Farm employment plummeted as a result.

At one time every Stewartry farm also had its own cheese-maker, until the craft became an industry centred on big creameries. Scotland's last ever dairyman/cheese-maker, and a national champion at that, was Bob Maxwell (1915-2006) of the Ross Farm on the west side of Kirkcudbright Bay. The last commercial cheese was made there in 1973.

The demise of the old land-based way of life is vividly reflected in the current death-throes of **'The Rural'**, the popular shorthand for the Scottish Women's Rural Institute. The idea of a women's equivalent to the Farmers' Institute was born in Canada in 1897 and quickly spread to Britain and Ireland.

When it began in Scotland in 1917, it was seen as part of the war effort at home and was backed by the Board of Agriculture in Scotland. Institutes spread throughout the country after the war for the promotion of productive housewifery. The Stewartry Federation of the SWRI was founded in 1922. Soon there was not a community in the county without its 'Rural'. The staple activities of the monthly meetings became the guest speaker with a didactic theme or practical advice, competitions in handicraft and home-cooking, and the rousing finale – the singing of the Rural Song. The movement flourished when most married women worked in the home, skilfully making the most of meagre resources.

The Rural has been rendered largely irrelevant by female emancipation, convenience food and inexpensive clothing that is not worth mending. The membership is elderly and largely unreplenished. As the members die off, so too do the organisations.

In addition to the effects of the milking-machine, continued streamlining and mechanisation – notably the tractor - have cleared the farmlands of much of their original population, and the land has become increasingly exploited as a resource for the leisure, tourism and retirement industries. Farmers, scunnered with the politics of food production and the stranglehold of the supermarket chains, convert the former workers' cottages into holiday lets and find that it is more worth their while to put caravans rather than cows on their lush pastoral acres. Shepherds end up running pony-rides. Dykers do ornamental work in the gardens of affluent retirees.

New trends in farm diversification

The Land and the Sea

One recreational resource of the Stewartry – the **hill country** of its heartland - was being appreciated long before the more concerted development of tourism. Big-time mountaineers and Munro-baggers may look down upon this clutch of the Southern Uplands, but closer inspection reveals a challenging awesomeness – not to mention a romantic remoteness and some of the most exciting and evocative upland nomenclature in the land. Take, for example, the western range known as The Awful Hand: the forefinger is Merrick (at 2766 feet, the county's highest peak); the other fingers are Shalloch on Minnoch, Tarfessock and Kirriereoch; and Benyellary is the thumb. Or take the parallel central Dungeon range: from Craiglee in the south through Craignaw, Craig Neldricken, Craignairny and Mullwharchar to Macaterick in the north - and in amongst them the 'Murder Hole', an inlet of Loch Neldricken made famous by the adventure yarns of S R Crockett (see Part 2 - The Novelists).

The Stewartry countryside is now, in one sense, being re-populated, but the new settlers are more likely to be making a living from a landline than from the land itself. Forget the fishing-net – rural Kirkcudbrightshire is run on the internet! The county has become a refuge for disillusioned city-dwellers, mainly from England. Some of them fulfil a fantasy of rural life by reviving village stores or running 'farmhouse bed and breakfast'. In some parts of the county, the Scots tongue is becoming a minority language.

   The area appears to be particularly attractive to devotees of 'alternative' lifestyles. It is ironic that vegan visionaries should find themselves looking out upon and admiring the drystane-dyked fields that were created for the husbanding of edible livestock. As the Stewartry is only marginally suitable for arable use, an animal-free vegan landscape in these parts would indeed be an eerie kind of wilderness.

The Celts, the Romans, the Angles, the Vikings, the Irish, the Anglo-Normans – the various invasions of people over the past two millennia have all left their mark. But the current plantation into the Stewartry of so many of its English neighbours may yet prove to be the most thoroughgoing of them all.

The Language

Many and bewilderingly varied have been the linguistic footprints passing across the Stewartry over the past two millennia. The original Celtic tongue of the Iron Age inhabitants (Brittonic or Cumbric, which survives as modern Welsh) was eventually replaced, from another Celtic source, by the Gaelic that crossed the water from Ireland with the settlers who created Dalriada, the kingdom that would eventually expand into Scotland as we now know it. In the intervening period, however, the Romans had brought their Latin (though it was never adopted by the natives), the Angles of Northumbria introduced an early form of English, and through the Viking raiders from Scandanavia a dash of Norse was dropped into the linguistic cocktail.

Ultimately the strongest language pressure came from the south. The Stewartry resisted the trend towards anglicisation longer than any other part of southern Scotland but, once the ancient Lordship of Galloway had been absorbed into a united Scotland by the 1230s, the Scottish monarchs' encouragement of southern immigration into the early medieval burghs proved decisive. The speech of the Stewartry became virtually indistinguishable from that of northern England. But then, as warfare and patriotism drove Scotland and England further apart during the thirteenth and fourteenth centuries, this northern English – known as 'Inglis' - diversified into two separate, though still closely related, languages. By the fifteenth century 'Inglis' north of the border had come to be known as 'Scotis' or, as we now say, Scots.

However, influences from the south were not long in reasserting themselves. The prestige of southern English writers such as Chaucer had a powerful effect on Scots literature. Then, in the 1560s, the leaders of the Scottish Reformation rejected the Latin of Roman Catholicism but failed to commission a Scots translation of the Bible. The adoption of the King James English version had a profound and pervasive effect. Now, to the ears of Scots folk, English appeared to have scriptural authority.

The final humiliation for the old Scots tongue came with the Union of the Crowns in 1603 when King James VI of Scotland became also King James I of England. The Scottish court disappeared south and the Scottish aristocracy found it expedient to adopt the speech of the London establishment, an affectation that afflicts the landed upper class of Scotland to this day. The Union of the Parliaments in 1707 confirmed the trend towards anglicisation, and the educated classes of Scotland expended much of

The Language

their intellectual energy through the eighteenth century in expunging so-called 'Scotticisms' from their English usage.

However, Scots stubbornly survived. While English became the official language, Scots remained, particularly in rural areas like the Stewartry, the language of first choice in everyday conversation, and writers like Robert Burns extended its range as far as it would go in the expression of strong feeling and satiric insight. But even Burns believed that his more serious thoughts should be couched in the grandiloquent cadences of Dr Johnson.

Today in the Stewartry the Scots-English dichotomy remains. A formal letter will be written in English, but a story told or a joke cracked in Scots. However, the linguistic choice is not a clear-cut one between two separate languages; what's available is an amazing range of registers within Scots and Scottish English. A Stewartry English-speaker has an extra vocabulary denied to an English English-speaker – and what follows is a flavour of the former for the enlightenment of the latter.

If you're a visitor to these parts, the locals will be very interested in where you *belong* [come from], where you *stay* [live], and whether it is *furth* [outside] of Scotland. They'll ask if you have any *weans* [children] and whether any of yours are *ages with* any of theirs. If anyone suggests meeting you at *denner-time*, don't think you have an evening appointment; that means lunch-time. Or it might be an arrangement for *the morn's morn* [tomorrow morning], let's say *the back o 10* [just after 10] in the *forenoon* [morning]. If you're a woman, don't be offended if you're addressed as *hen*; it's meant in the nicest possible way.

If you're dissatisfied with the standard of your accommodation, you might like to complain that it's *clartie* [dirty] or *foosty* [smelling of mould]. But try not to *girn* [grumble] too much or create a *stooshie* [quarrel], otherwise you might cause a *carfuffle* [disturbance] and get yourself into a *fankle* [mess]. After all, you wouldn't want to be thought of as being *carnaptious* [disagreeable]. When you sign the visitors' book, it'll be noticed if you are *corriefisted* [left-handed]. A *left-footer*, by the way, is a Roman Catholic. If you have tea-making facilities in your room, you'll be able to *mask* [brew] it yourself, though if you don't leave it long enough the result might be *peelie-wallie* [weak].

Instead of just *plitterin aboot* [pottering about], you might take a *dauner* [stroll] down the street for *the messages* [errands], including some *baps* [rolls] from the baker. While there, check out the *bridies* [pasties] and *tattie-scones* [potato-cakes], and be aware that the *crumpets* may not be what you're used to. Pop into the fishmonger's to inspect the *haddies* [haddock] and *queenies* [scallops]; and into the butcher's to find out what he means by *potted hough* [jellied meat mould], a *gigot* [leg of lamb], *pope's eye steak* [rump], and *links* [sausages]. If not cooking for yourself, try a *carry-out* [takeaway], perhaps a *fish supper* from the chip shop or just a *poke* [bag] of chips, followed by a pint of *heavy* [bitter].

Let's hope the weather is not too *dreich* [dull], leaving you *chitterin* [shivering] in a *smirr* [drizzly sea-mist], and that you don't get *drookit* [wet]. Just in case it's chilly, remember to bring your *simmit* [vest]. If it's not too cold at the *shore* [beach], you'll be able to have a *dook* [paddle or swim]. To keep warm and stop yourself being *scunnered* [fed up], you could join the kids in a game of *peevers* [hopscotch]. To cheer yourself up, you might like a *wee refreshment* [a euphemism for alcohol], but *mind* [remember] that if you go *on the randan* [paint the town red] you might end up *fou* or *steamin* [drunk] and feel *wabbit* [worn out] in the morning.

As you go around the Stewartry, you'll maybe get a *keek* [look] at a *tolbooth* [early town-hall]; an *academy* [secondary school], where the headteacher is the *Rector* and the caretaker is the *jannie*; and a *Sheriff Court* with its *procurator-fiscal* [prosecutor] and the *not proven* verdict. You'll find various *kirks* [churches]. The Presbyterian one is led by a *minister* who lives in a *manse*. Worshippers at the Episcopal church are known as *piskies*.

Among the glories of the surrounding countryside and its *clachans* [hamlets] are the *drystane dykes* [stone walls without mortar] and the *Belties* [black Galloway cattle with a band of white round the middle]. Note in the fields how common *mowdie-hills* [mole-hills] are. Local geographical terms include *loch* [lake], *haugh* [low-lying ground close to a river], *firth* [as in Solway Firth] and *clints* (steep rocks). Bird-watchers will be on the look-out for a *laverock* [skylark], a *mavis* [song-thrush] and a *whaup* [curlew].

You might meet some *kenspeckle* [well-known and colourful] characters. You'll find a pleasantly *easy-oasy* attitude to life. Someone might invite you round to *my bit* [home]. *Chap* [knock] the door when you arrive. No one will let you sit in a pub alone: you'll be urged to *come into the body o the kirk*. You're unlikely to find anyone being *crabbit* [bad-tempered] with you. If, however, anyone wishes to insult you, there's no shortage of terms of abuse: *gowk, bawheid, dunderheid, tumshieheid, bampot, gomeril, blatherskite, galoot, galumph* and *nyaff*, to name but a few.

After your visit, it'll be *back tae auld claes and porridge* [dull normality]. But it's not such a *sair fecht* [hard life]. You can *aye* [always] return. As we say in the Stewartry, *cheeribye* – and *haste ye back*!

The Pirate

The Stewartry's most celebrated native personality was in fact an enemy of the British State. John Paul Jones (1747-1792) left these shores at the age of thirteen, only ever returned to wreak havoc, and ended up being feted as 'The Founder of the American Navy'. In the USA he is revered as a national hero. Back home in south-west Scotland, he is presented as a swashbuckling character, his adventurous life commemorated in a dedicated museum at his birthplace, Kirkbean.

He began life as the son of a gardener on the Arbigland estate. Then he was just John Paul; the Jones was added later to help avoid arrest at the height of his notoriety. After a seaman's apprenticeship based at Whitehaven on the English side of the Solway Firth, he found better employment prospects on the other side of the Atlantic. At the outbreak of the American War of Independence in 1775 he opted to align himself with the colonial insurgents. He was eventually given command of a warship called the *Ranger*.

In 1778 Jones and his crew set sail for the UK, with the aim of terrorising the coastal communities of the land he had rejected and capturing hostages who could be exchanged for American prisoners of war. Where better to try his luck than the coast he

An artist's impression of the *Ranger*

had come to know so well in boyhood? He headed for Kirkcud-bright, where he had once been held in the Tolbooth on suspicion of murder until he was able to prove his innocence.

He anchored the *Ranger* off St Mary's Isle, the Kirkcudbright estate of the Earl of Selkirk. The plan was to take the earl as a high-profile captive. Unfortunately for Jones, the earl was away from home. Jones was all for retreating in disappointment, but his crewmen were hungry for booty and the master sensed that, without reward, they would be in a mood for mutiny. Not wishing to be seen by the Countess as a blackguard, Jones hung back and let his men get on with it. With exemplary politeness on both sides, the Selkirk family silver was handed over. Later, Jones bought the silver from his men and sent it back to the Countess with a florid explanation of his motives:

> Though I have drawn my sword in the present generous struggle for the rights of men, yet I am not in arms as an American nor am I in pursuit of riches. My fortune is liberal enough, having no wife nor family, and having lived long enough to know that riches cannot insure happiness. I profess myself a citizen of the world, totally unfettered by the little mean distinctions of climate or of country, which diminish the benevolence of the heart and set bounds to philanthropy.

Jones' most daring escapade was aboard the *Bonhomme Richard* in 1779. Off Flamborough Head he engaged a convoy of merchant ships and their naval escorts in a sea battle of such ferocity that even Jones' own ship had to be abandoned. Jones emerged victorious, transferring his command to the principal British frigate.

All the while Jones was becoming an international celebrity. In Paris, where the French authorities were supportive of the breakaway states across the Atlantic, he was the toast of the salons and lionised by high-class women. Louis XVI honoured him with a military award and with the title of 'Chevalier'. A bust of him was made by the sculptor Jean-Antoine Houdon.

The Houdon bust
at the US Naval Academy

The Pirate

Jones' fame brought him to the attention of Catherine The Great, the tsarina of Russia, and when the War of Independence ended and Jones was left with no role, she hired him to help in the fight against the Turks. He performed heroically, but he made enemies within the Russian establishment and took his leave in 1789.

His naval career was effectively at an end, and he nursed a grievance that no country had allowed his potential to be fulfilled. In the remaining three years of his life he wandered around Europe, ending up back in Paris. Amazingly, despite so recently having been regarded by the British as a traitor, his travels took him to London where he was greeted as a great man and dined at aristocratic tables. He even met Lord Daer, son of his would-be hostage the Earl of Selkirk. They chatted amiably for an hour or two, and later Daer told his father that Jones 'seems a sensible little fellow. He is not as dark as I had heard'.

Another astonishing feature of his visit to England was his being invited to the naval dockyard at Portsmouth. The officers were awe-struck by his presence. 'I felt particularly complimented,' Jones wrote in his journal, 'at the assiduity with which these young officers plied me with questions about the Russian and French navies...' One of them had fought against him twelve years earlier in the infamous battle off Flamborough Head.

Although welcomed back to England as a celebrity, he appears never to have re-visited his birthplace. He did, however, keep in touch with two sisters. Towards the end of his life, when he was otherwise occupied by his declining health, he was disappointed to hear that the sisters had badly fallen out, and he pleaded for family unity:

> I shall not conceal from you that your family discord aggravates infinitely all my pains. My grief is inexpressible that two sisters whose happiness is equally so interesting to me do not live in that mutual tenderness and affection which would do so much honour to themselves and to the memory of their worthy parents.

The recklessness of his sea-going lifestyle had taken its toll on his health and, additionally, he contracted jaundice. He died alone in his Paris lodgings on 18 July 1792, aged 45. When his body was found, the face was pressed into the bed, his feet on the floor. Though not a religious man, he may at the end have been praying.

He was buried in a cemetery for foreign Protestants, and his body remained there until 1905 when, on the orders of the American President, it was exhumed and ceremoniously taken to the USA. Jones' remains now lie in the chapel crypt of the US Naval Academy in Annapolis – a stunning apotheosis for the son of a Kirkbean gardener.

The John Paul Jones 'shrine' at Kirkbean

The Hydro

Art in Concrete, Charles Oppenheimer's take on the Hydro scheme

The Galloway Hydro-Electric Scheme is a spectacular partnership of natural forces and human ingenuity stretching right down the middle of the Stewartry from the northern hills near Carsphairn to Tongland close to where the River Dee enters the Solway Firth. It was a boldly imaginative and pioneering undertaking, Scotland's first scheme of its kind for public supply. Today the Stewartry can be proud of having been so 'green' at such an early stage. Not that it seemed 'green' to everyone at the time. The heritage lobby was indignant. An editorial in *The Gallovidian Annual* of 1929 warned its readers of the impending threat to this 'land of sweetness and harmony':

> ...when the time came to defend her, to preserve this beauty and harmony, scarce a voice was raised within her borders. Where there should have been united effort and solid opposition on the part of her land-owners and her administrators there was apathy and slackness, and worse. Some of those who should have been hottest in her defence were associated instead with the promoters of the scheme that was so adversely to affect her beauty – a scheme which was conceived and launched and had gone through Parliament almost before the greater proportion of the people of Galloway knew anything about it.

The idea of harnessing the Stewartry's natural waterways to produce electricity began to be taken seriously in the early 1920s.

At first the engineers thought a scheme for Galloway alone would be prohibitively expensive. The situation changed with the establishment in 1926 of the national grid. The opportunity for surplus Stewartry power to be exported to the rest of the country changed the economics of the plan. In 1929 an enabling bill passed through Parliament. Work began in 1931 and lasted some five years.

One of eight Hydro dams

There are six power stations, eight dams and numerous tunnels, aqueducts and pipelines. Here is how it works, going from north to south. Loch Doon, on the border with Ayrshire, is the main storage reservoir. When supplies are low, the loch can be topped up via a tunnel from the Water of Deugh and the Bow Burn. When water is required for the power stations further down the valley, it is released from Loch Doon through the Drumjohn needle valve. The force of this release is so great that it was decided no longer to waste it, so in the mid-1980s Drumjohn got a mini power station of its own.

Going south, the first three of the original 1930s stations all have their own dams: Kendoon, Carsfad and Earlstoun. The next station, Glenlee, is fed from the Clatteringshaws reservoir to its west through a three-and-a-half-mile-long tunnel.

The final section is Loch Ken-Glenlochar-Tongland. The loch is the storage reservoir for Tongland station, the flow of water southwards being controlled by the Glenlochar barrage with its six lifting sluice-gates.

It was a huge construction project, employing at its height some fifteen hundred workers for whom temporary camps were set up. Two extra police officers were stationed in the area. It was a time of high unemployment and men came from all over the country in search of jobs, causing some resentment among the local unemployed.

Much of the work was dangerous. During a six-month period in 1933, five workers were killed and sixteen seriously injured in the excavation of the feeder tunnel from Clatteringshaws to Glenlee.

The Hydro

Today we admire the power stations' Art Deco facades, and marvel that the reservoirs, dams and turbines are still productive after three-quarters of a century. Although now the structures seem wholly integrated into the landscape, the development radically altered many features of the countryside. Loch Doon had its natural outflow towards Ayrshire altered; the castle in the middle of the loch would have been submerged by the raising of the water level, so it was removed stone by stone and re-built at its present location on the western fringe of the loch. The reservoir at Clatteringshaws was created by placing a dam across the Blackwater of Dee to flood adjacent marshland.

Steps were taken to minimise the impact on wildlife. Four fish ladders with resting pools were created to enable salmon to return to their spawning grounds, though salmon enthusiasts maintain that the measures are insufficiently effective. Since 1996 the scheme's operators have cooperated with the Royal Society for the Protection of Birds to ensure that the water level of Loch Ken is appropriate during the breeding season.

In 1938 a memorial was unveiled to the engineer William McLellan by company chairman Lord Meston, who said:

> In the execution of this work, hands have had to be laid upon the beauties of the country. Power houses, dams, aqueducts, surge towers now dot the valley and it will take time for them to merge into the hues and contours of the landscape, but in at least a partial compensation a whole series of new lochs have been created which will grow in attractiveness as nature takes them into its care.

Clatteringshaws reservoir

In the same year, though, W G M Dobie took a different view and put it in verse in *The Modern Raiders* [a reference to S R Crockett's Stewartry novel *The Raiders*]:

> A raider comes today who kills
> The glories of our glens and hills
> With unheroic Acts and Bills
> And 'private legislation':
> The company promoter's pen
> Will dam the Deugh and dam the Ken
> And dam the Dee – oh, damn the men
> Who plan such desecration!

A couple of decades earlier Loch Doon had been earmarked for another kind of development, but it all ended in the ignominy of what became known as **'The Loch Doon Scandal'**. During the First World War, the defence authorities decided the loch would be an ideal site for the creation of an aerial gunnery practice facility. The targets were to move in a zig-zagging fashion along a mono-rail to be built on the slopes to the east of the loch, and seaplanes would land on the loch itself.

A huge construction programme, involving 3000 workers at its height, was started. But, after enormous expenditure, the whole enterprise was abandoned. The advice of locals, who had pointed out that the loch was frozen over for much of the year, was vindi-cated. A parliamentary inquiry into the waste of resources con-cluded that the grandiose scheme 'was misconceived from the beginning'.

Loch Doon Castle in its new location

The Bards

Scotland's 'national bard' **Robert Burns** (1759-96) was, of course, an Ayrshireman but he knew the Stewartry well, being familiar with the Solway coast through his work as an excise officer based in Dumfries. However, when, on July 27, 1793, he went westwards over the Nith, mounted on a grey Highland sheltie and accompanied by his friend and Dumfries neighbour John Syme, it was for pleasure.

They passed through Parton on the way to their first lodgings with the Gordons of Kenmure Castle at the head of Loch Ken, where they stayed for three days. Viscount Kenmure took them on an entertaining boat trip down the loch along with some other passengers, including the parish minister, the Rev John Gillespie. Their destination was Airds Hill, to view an arbour created by a local poet John Lowe, author of the popular sentimental ballad *Mary's Dream*. However, the craft grounded short of where they intended to land. Kenmure scrambled ashore and encouraged the others to follow. The minister said he would just wait for their return. But Burns jumped into the water and manoeuvred the elderly cleric onto his shoulder. Syme is reputed to have exclaimed: 'Well, Burns, of all men on earth, you are the last I would have expected to see *priest-ridden*'. According to the source of this story, Burns was not amused by the remark.

Wherever the famous poet went, he was called upon to extemporise verses for the occasion. Viscountess Kenmure requested an epitaph for her recently deceased dog Echo, and Burns obligingly sang for his supper:

> In wood and wild, ye warbling throng,
> Your heavy loss deplore;
> Now half extinct your powers of Song,
> Sweet Echo is no more.
>
> Ye jarring, screeching things around,
> Scream your discordant joys;
> Now half your din of tuneless sound
> With Echo silent lies.

Leaving Kenmure Castle, Burns and Syme set off for Gate-house of Fleet, making the westward journey across bleak moor-land. They got soaked in a violent storm. According to Syme, '... we were utterly wet and we got vengeance at Gatehouse by get-ting utterly drunk...'

Legend has it that Burns wrote *Scots Wha Hae* while in Gate-house, and to this day the management of the Murray Arms Hotel continue to claim that he did so on their premises. There is plenty of evidence to suggest that he did no such thing.

The following morning, as they headed for Kirkcudbright, Burns was in the foul mood of a man with a severe hangover, and his temper got worse when he ripped his new, but by now very damp, boots by trying to force them onto his feet. 'Mercy on me how he did fume and rage,' reported his companion.

They were due to have lunch at the home of a man by the name of Dalzell. Syme had arranged it, but the venue had to be switched to the inn where they were staying because, according to Syme, 'Burns' obstreperous independence would not dine but where he should, as he said, eat like a Turk, drink like a fish and swear like the Devil'.

The highlight of their visit to Kirkcudbright was an evening spent at the home of the Earl of Selkirk on his St Mary's Isle estate to the south of the town. The Earl had another distinguished guest that evening. He was Pietro Urbani, an Italian musicologist who had come to live in Scotland because of his enthusiasm for the country's song tradition. The company were enchanted by this chance meeting. Urbani sang for them, while Burns recited his *Lord Gregory*. Of Burns's moving performance, Syme wrote: 'such was the effect, that a dead silence ensued...' The next day Burns and his friend returned to Dumfries.

Another Stewartry hostelry lays claim to being the location of a Burns composition. The Selkirk Arms Hotel in Kirkcudbright adver-tises itself as the place where he wrote *The Selkirk Grace*:

> Some hae meat and canna eat
> And some wad eat that want it;
> But we hae meat, and we can eat,
> Sae let the Lord be thankit.

Modern scholarship, however, now casts doubt on this being the work of Burns. The editors of The Canongate Burns (2001) place it among Undetermined and Rejected Works, explaining: 'This is rejected because evidence suggests that it existed as a Galloway Covenanter Grace long before Burns. Hearsay evidence that Burns *recited* an English version of the Grace during his Galloway tour is no evidence for composition'. They add tartly: 'This rather docile, uncontroversial grace has managed to reserve itself a ritualistic recital in the Burns cult at annual Suppers worldwide'.

Burns and Syme had another excursion to the Stewartry in 1794, this time venturing as far west as Kirroughtree, where they were guests of the laird Patrick Heron. Although he enjoyed the attention his celebrity brought, Burns remained touchy about mixing with toffs and, shortly before the visit, wrote to David McCulloch of Ardwall near Gatehouse of Fleet, seeking his help: '…let me remind you of your kind promise to accompany me there. I will need all the friends I can muster, for I am indeed ill at ease whenever I approach your Honorables & Right Honorables'.

Syme would have had his own reservations about Heron, for his father lost a fortune in the collapse of a bank of which Heron had been one of the founders. However, the meeting seems to have gone satisfactorily, for the following year Burns did Heron a big favour: he wrote comic ballads in support of Heron as Whig candidate in the parliamentary election:

> Then let us drink - The Stewartry,
> Kerroughtree's laird, and a' that,
> Our representative to be,
> For weel he's worthy a' that.
> For a' that, and a' that.
> Here's Heron yet for a' that!
> A House of Commons such as he,
> They wad be blest that saw that.

William Nicholson

At one time every Stewartry community had its resident versifiers, homespun bards celebrating local characters and comic incidents. Most of them have sunk into obscurity. **William Nicholson** (1783-1849) is the one who still stands out. He was born in the parish of Borgue, one of eight children. He was inattentive at school, but received from his mother a passion for the old ballads and legends of the Stewartry. He earned a living, fitfully, as a pedlar, but his welcome in the far-flung farming cottages was more for his recitations and performances with the bagpipes.

In 1813, with a portfolio of his own poems, he set off to Edinburgh and there, with the encouragement of the 'Ettrick Shepherd'

James Hogg, his first collection was published. Back home, he was feted as a celebrity. But the socialising that the fame entailed aggravated his dependence on alcohol, and his health deteriorated. He began having delusions, and during one spell of mental enfeeblement he travelled to London seeking – in vain – an audience with the King.

Another edition of his poems in 1827 revived his fortunes for a while, but the drink-fuelled spiral of decline resumed. When he died in 1849, he was a pauper. A commentator summed up his final phase thus:

> ...he fell into dissipated habits, playing at fairs and markets
> as a sort of gaberlunzie [beggar], the grave at last closing
> in gloom over the ruins of a man of real genius.

Nicholson was buried at Kirkandrews. Before his death, he had his portrait painted by the distinguished Gatehouse of Fleet artist John Faed. Based on that portrait, a commemorative plaque was erected at the school in Borgue.

Nicholson's most famous poem is *The Brownie of Blednoch*, a racy tale of Aiken-drum, a supernatural being of awesome ugliness ('there's a hole where a nose should hae been'), who suddenly appears looking for employment.

> I trow the bauldest stood aback,
> Wi' a gape and a glower till their lugs did crack,
> As the shapeless phantom mum'ling spak,
>   'Hae ye wark for Aiken-drum?'

> O! had ye seen the bairns' fright,
> As they stared at this wild and unyirthly wight,
> As he stauket in 'tween the dark and the light,
>   And graned out, 'Aiken-drum!'

In more recent times the Stewartry has by no means been overwhelmed by bardic talent. One of its most interesting poets **William Neill** was a settler from Ayrshire. Born at Prestwick in 1922, Neill was a 'late developer' as a literary man. He was almost 50 when his first book was published.

His original career was with the RAF. Later he went to Edinburgh University as a mature student, specialising in Celtic Studies and English. He set out to write in all three of Scotland's languages: Gaelic, Scots and English. In 1969 he was the Bard at the Gaelic Mod. He came to the Stewartry to teach at Castle Douglas High School and he set up home in the nearby village of Crossmichael.

The Bards

In *Galloway Landscape and Other Poems* (1981), the title
poem addresses the controversial plan of the late 1970s to use
the Galloway hills as a deep-bore dumping-ground for nuclear
waste:

> I walk on rough thin roads with passing places.
>
> Nobody passes. A grey mist trails its cloak
> over dead covenanter and dragoon
> shriven of their past quarrels;
> prelacy versus presbytery
> fires no contention now.
> A new, more worldly disputation
> has come to boulder and rock,
> to compass of cairn and loch.
>
> Now we have learned to worship uniformly;
> from the unknowable nothingness
> of fissioned atoms
> all things should be made new.
> Yet some, well-versed in older legends, know
> fulfilment cannot come without a sting.
> How shall we choose the gift, avoid the aftermath?
>
> The dark hills give no answer.
> Prelacy and plutonium are all one
> to their uncaring granite.

The Novelists

The Stewartry's outstanding (and just about only) native novelist was **Samuel Rutherford Crockett** (1859-1914). His early childhood was spent on the farm of Little Duchrae in the parish of Balmaghie. His mother was unmarried, and they lived with his maternal grandparents and three uncles. The household was devoutly Christian, his grandparents belonging to the fundamentalist Presbyterians known as the Cameronians (though they were surprisingly non-judgmental about their daughter's carnal lapse).

A magazine caricature of S R Crockett

Crockett's first school was in the village of Laurieston. When he was seven, the family moved to Cotton Street in Castle Douglas ('Cairn Edward' in his novels), where he attended the Free Church School. His class-mates included William MacGeorge who would later become a well-known painter.

Crockett studied literature at Edinburgh University. At first he wanted to become a journalist, and went to London to explore the possibilities. But he was still under the influence of his religious upbringing and opted to return to university and train as a minister in the Free Church of Scotland. Before the call of the kirk, however, he had seen much of Europe as a tutor to rich youngsters sent on the Grand Tour. While he and one of his pupils were mountaineering in the Tyrol, Crockett unexpectedly met the German Chancellor Bismarck:

> ...we learnt that Bismarck was staying in the little Tyrol village where we put up. Everyone was talking about the 'mad Englanders' who climbed hills in the winter, and Bismarck sent an *aide* to ask us to call on him, just as we were, ice-axes and all. He was extremely civil, and when he heard that we were thinking of going to Heidelberg to study he gave us a letter of introduction to 'all officials of the German Empire' asking them to do all they could for us.

181

Crockett's first parish post, from 1886, was at Penicuik in Mid-lothian. By then he had given himself his middle name in homage to the seventeenth-century Presbyterian diehard Samuel Ruther-ford (see Part 1 - Anwoth).

All the time, however, he had been writing. His first published book was a collection of poems *Dulce Cor*. But it was with prose that he made his name. In 1893 *The Stickit Minister*, a collection of short stories, was published. He dedicated it to Robert Louis Ste-venson. Stevenson responded by writing a poem for Crockett evoking the history of the Stewartry and his own impending death (see Part 1 - Laurieston).

Though they never met, Crockett and Stevenson became friends through their correspondence. When Stevenson received his first letter from Crockett, the handwriting was hard to decipher and Stevenson wrote back: 'DEAR MINISTER OF THE FREE KIRK AT PENICUIK, - For O, man, I cannae read your name!...' Stevenson ended by rebuking Crockett for putting NB in his ad-dress: 'Don't put 'NB' in your paper: put Scotland, and be done with it. The name of my native land is not NORTH BRITAIN, what-ever may be the name of yours.'

The Stickit Minister was an instant success, and in 1894 two novels followed: *The Raiders* (about eighteenth-century smugglers along the Stewartry coast) and *The Lilac Sunbonnet* (a love story in which religious bigotry is mocked). Crockett by this time was in demand – for more books, for articles, for public appearances; and he was finding it increasingly difficult to cope with the competing demands of his pastoral role. Finally, after a fearsome struggle with his Cameronian conscience, he decided in 1895 to resign from the ministry and devote himself full-time to writing. From the pulpit he explained his decision to his parishioners:

> Most sincerely do I believe that the same Lord who sent me here to preach the Gospel has revealed to me the posses-sion of a talent which He desires and intends me to use. I did not seek this literary work – it found me. I have only followed on, wondering often, doubting often, and yet sure that to every faithful servant there is given no tool which the Master Workman does not intend him to use.

Crockett contentedly became an ordinary parishioner under his successor, with whom he got on well. But some of the more big-oted kirk members thought he was a disgrace for having rejected God's ministry to become a mere writer of fiction. They doubtless would have also disapproved of the way his fame brought him into touch with the celebrities of the literary and artistic world.

It is an indication of Crockett's fame in his own lifetime that in 1896 he sat for the painter Whistler, but, owing to the death of the artist's wife, the work was put aside and Crockett appears not to have taken up a later invitation from Whistler to complete the sittings in Paris.

In 1906 Crockett moved to Peebles, where his new home had to have a library added on to accommodate his vast collection of books: he is reckoned to have accumulated between thirty and forty thousand volumes.

Though he was tall, handsome, athletic and apparently strong, Crockett's health was weak. Increasingly in later life he fled from the Scottish winters in search of Mediterranean sunshine. His wife Ruth and their four children were usually left behind. These therapeutic periods of exile were tinged with loneliness. When he was home during the summer he often spent time in Auchencairn at the house of his uncle, which he eventually inherited.

He died in April 1914 at Tarascon near Avignon. The coffin was carried through Castle Douglas to the tolling of the town bell, and he was buried exactly where he had wanted, four miles away in the kirkyard of his native Balmaghie (see Part 1 - Glenlochar).

Crockett created a prodigious output - over 50 books - but none of the later novels had the freshness of his early bestsellers. *The Raiders* remains popular, with its cracking pace from the very first sentence: 'It was upon Rathan Head that I first heard their bridle-reins jingling clear.'

Crockett's reputation has suffered through association with the 'Kailyard [cabbage-patch] School' of Scottish novelists, a sneering term for late-Victorian writers specialising in couthie, sentimental rural themes rather than confronting the gritty issues of urban industrial living. Though he never returned except for holidays, his first attachment remained to his native county: its history and its rural way of life as he had experienced it in his idyllic childhood. *Raiderland* (1904) is a compendium of his writings about Galloway. His most popular novel has left its stamp across the Stewartry: there's a Raiders Bridge and a forest drive called The Raiders Road; and a New Galloway grocer Robert Cowan used to be very proud of his Raiders blend of tea.

There are numerous Stewartry connections with the novels of **Sir Walter Scott** (1771-1832), but scenes set in the area cannot be read as authentic descriptions. Although Scott knew neighbouring Dumfriesshire fairly well, his direct experience of Kirkcudbrightshire was limited, if not non-existent.

The Novelists

Sir Walter Scott

As a lawyer, Scott represented the Rev McNaught, minister of Girthon, south-east of Gatehouse of Fleet, who was convicted by the General Assembly of the Church of Scotland on various charges of inappropriate conduct, including drunkenness, flirtation and the singing of lewd songs. Scott may have visited the Stewartry in 1793 for a consultation with his client, but the possibility is hotly disputed by Scott scholars.

Most of Scott's information about the region came from his friend Joseph Train, a local antiquarian. Train fed him with stories and legends. *Guy Mannering* (1815) is partly about smuggling on the Solway coast. The name of the principal smuggling character Dirk Hatteraick has been attached to two caves, one near Kirkcudbright, the other close to Carsluith, but neither is specifically the cave as described in the story.

A hotel in Creetown is named after the Ellangowan estate in the novel with no particular justification. Ellangowan Castle in the novel was more identifiable with Caerlaverock Castle in Dumfriesshire. The gypsy character Meg Merrilies so entranced the poet John Keats that when he walked across the Stewartry he believed he was in 'Meg Merrilies country' (see Other Pairs of Eyes).

The other major Scott novel aided by Train's Stewartry stories was *Old Mortality* (1816). 'Old Mortality' was Robert Paterson, the stonemason who devoted himself to carving memorials for the Covenanting 'martyrs' (see Part 1 - Balmaclellan).

The most celebrated twentieth-century novel to have the Stewartry as one of its settings is *The Thirty-Nine Steps* (1915) by the Borderer **John Buchan** (1875-1940). His descriptions of the hills and moorlands around the Gatehouse of Fleet area were well grounded in close personal observation.

As a young man, he was a frequent visitor to the region and a lover of its hills. According to his autobiography, he once covered sixty-three miles in a single walking expedition in the area.

While studying at Oxford, Buchan often visited Ardwall near Gatehouse of Fleet, home of the eminent lawyer Andrew Jameson, Lord Ardwall, whose son Johnnie was a university contemporary of Buchan's. In his 1913 biography of Lord Ardwall, Buchan wrote of these youthful visits:

John Buchan

> Our amusements were peculiar. We would return in the small hours of the morning from expeditions to the Dungeon of Buchan, and go to bed in broad daylight; or we would indulge in the precarious game of swimming horses across the Fleet at high tide, or the still more precarious sport - a Jameson patent - of pursuing hares on horseback with a greyhound over the briar-clad dykes and bogs of a Galloway moor. It is a marvel that our necks remained unbroken; perhaps they were spared for that judicial end which the Sheriff prophesised.

In *The Thirty-Nine Steps* Buchan's hero Richard Hannay, in flight from the skulduggery of a foreign spy-ring, arrives at Dumfries railway station – 'just in time to bundle out and get into the slow Galloway train'. He shares a third-class compartment with hill farmers returning from the market 'in an atmosphere of shag and clay pipes'. They had 'lunched heavily and were highly flavoured with whisky.'

He gets off at a remote moorland station, probably Gatehouse of Fleet, and begins to feel the calming effect of the Stewartry:

> It was a gorgeous spring evening, with every hill showing as clear as a cut amethyst. The air had the queer, rooty smell of bogs, but it was as fresh as mid-ocean, and it had the strangest effect on my spirits. I actually felt light-hearted. I might have been a boy out for a spring holiday tramp, instead of a man of thirty-seven very much wanted by the police. I swung along that road whistling. There was no plan of campaign in my head, only just to go on and on in this blessed, honest-smelling hill country, for every mile put me in better humour with myself.

The Stewartry features in another Buchan thriller, *Castle Gay* (1930), which centres on a Fleet Street press baron, but he changes the name of the county to the Canonry.

The Novelists

Dorothy L Sayers

Dorothy L Sayers (1893-1957) was another non-native novelist able to write about the Stewartry with authority. She and her husband 'Mac' Fleming, a journalist and amateur artist, knew Kirkcudbright and its vicinity well from regular holidays there. At first they stayed at the Anwoth Hotel in Gatehouse of Fleet. Then, in 1929, they established a base of their own at 14a High Street, Kirkcudbright. They were at the heart of the town's then flourishing artists' colony, which provided her with the background for *Five Red Herrings* (1931).

Her posh amateur sleuth Lord Peter Wimsey investigates an artist's suspicious death; most of the other leading painters are suspects. She is said to have got the idea for the book after quarrelling with a real-life artist in Kirkcudbright. A friend said: 'Why don't you go and write a book and murder him in it?'

The story is actually rather tiresome, a puzzle revolving around the intricacies of railway timetables. The Scottish Colourist S J Peploe, working in Kirkcudbright when the book came out, wrote to his wife: 'I am trying to read *Five Red Herrings.* What a silly, dull book - full of padding. I fear I won't finish it'. There are, however, passages with authentic period flavour:

> The artistic centre of Galloway is Kirkcudbright, where the painters form a scattered constellation, whose nucleus is the High Street, and whose outer stars twinkle in remote hillside cottages, radiating brightness as far as Gatehouse-of-Fleet. There are large and stately studios, panelled and high, in strong stone houses filled with gleaming brass and polished oak. There are workaday studios - summer perching-places rather than settled homes - where a good north light and a litter of brushes and canvas form the whole artistic stock-in-trade. There are little homely studios, gay with blue and red and yellow curtains and odd scraps of pottery, tucked away down narrow closes and adorned with gardens, where old-fashioned flowers riot in the rich and friendly soil. There are studios that are simply and solely barns, made beautiful by ample proportions and high-pitched rafters, and habitable by the addition of a tortoise stove and a gas-ring. There are artists who have large families and keep domestics in cap and apron; artists who engage rooms, and are taken care of by landladies; artists who live in couples or alone, with a woman who comes in to clean; artists who live hermit-like and do their own char-ring. There are painters in oils, painters in water-colour, painters in pastel, etchers and illustrators, workers in metal;

artists of every variety, having this one thing in common—that they take their work seriously and have no time for amateurs.

By the late 1920s the rather masculine figure of this celebrity writer - often wearing a sombrero-style hat (though sometimes a bowler, complete with collar and tie) and smoking through a cigarette-holder - had become a familiar sight in the town. Her wider renown ensured that the book went straight into the bestsellers list and was reprinted within weeks. It brought the Stewartry to the attention of the outside world and gave a modest boost to the tourist trade, as Sayers wryly observed in a letter to her publisher:

> ...people arrive in Gatehouse and Kirkcudbright and say they've come to spend their holidays there because they read a book called *Five Red Herrings*. Whereupon the proprietor says: 'Och aye? Weel, the authoress is jist stayin' in Gallowa' the noo - maybe ye'd like tae be meetin' her.' So presently I am displayed as one of the local amenities, and the visitor says: 'Now, I've just bought a copy of your book - I wonder if you would write your name in it for me.' Which I do.

Five Red Herrings was dedicated to Joe Dignam, proprietor of the Anwoth Hotel in Gatehouse of Fleet ('kindliest of landlords'):

> Dear Joe,
> Here at last is your book about Gatehouse and Kirkcudbright. All the places are real places and all the trains are real trains, and all the landscapes are correct, except that I have run up a few new houses here and there. But you know better than anybody that none of the people are in the least like the real people, and that no Galloway artist would ever think of getting intoxicated or running away from his wife or bashing a fellow-citizen over the head. All that is just put in for the fun and to make it more exciting.
> ...please tell Provost Laurie that though this story is laid in the petrol-gas period, I have not forgotten that Gatehouse will now have its electric light by which to read this book.
> ...tell Mrs Dignam that we shall come back next summer to eat some more potato-scones at the Anwoth.

A year before *Five Red Herrings*, another detective novel featuring both the Stewartry and its railway system was published: *Sir John Magill's Last Journey* by **Freeman Wills Crofts** (1879-1957). Crofts was a Northern Irish railway engineer before taking up full-time writing in 1929. Many of his yarns centred on Inspector

The Novelists

French of Scotland Yard. In this one, Sir John Magill, a wealthy Belfast businessman, is on his way home from London on the Euston-Stranraer sleeper train connecting with the ferry for Ireland. He disappears during the journey. The investigation takes Inspector French to various locations in south-west Scotland, including Castle Douglas and Kirkandrews near Borgue.

Interestingly, Crofts' book gets a playful mention in Sayers'. A suspect, questioned by the Kirkcudbrightshire chief constable Sir Maxwell Jamieson about his whereabouts at the time of the death under investigation, describes the spot where he was painting, the picnic he had, and the book he was reading at the time:

> ' - a very nice book, all about a murder committed in this part of the country. *Sir John Magill's Last Journey,* by one Mr Crofts. You should read it. The police in that book called in Scotland Yard to solve their problems for them.'
> Sir Maxwell took this information without wincing…

In *Ritchie, or Behind the Tartan Curtain* (1954), a comic novel by **John P Barter**, art expert Raphael Thomas is asked by a London Bond Street dealer Emery Chavasse to go to the Stewartry to evaluate a bust attributed to Leonardo. But Raphael dislikes the Scots, too many of whom he encounters in London, and requires a lot of persuasion to take on the commission.

> 'It's impossible to escape them. I'm always running into them. They're everywhere, with their ...'
> 'Then Kirkcudbrightshire is the place for you.'
> 'But it's in the middle of Scotland! What a mad way to pronounce it: Kercoobry!'
> 'It is rather strange. However, listen to this.'
> 'I'm listening, but nothing will convince me.'
> 'The area of Kirkcudbrightshire is about eight hundred and ninety-nine square miles. The number of people living in it, whom we may presume to be mostly Scotch, is slightly over thirty thousand.'
> 'Well?'
> 'That makes about thirty-three of them to the square mile.'
> 'Quite enough.'
> 'Now the area of London is one hundred and seventeen square miles...the number of Scots reputed to dwell in London is two hundred thousand.'
> 'Good God! Is it as many as that?'
> 'At *least*. There may be more. That makes – what do you think? – over one thousand seven hundred to each square mile of London.'

'It sounds fantastic, and yet I can almost believe it.'

'By comparing the figures, you will see that your chances of encountering a Scot in London are approximately fifty-one times as great as they would be in Kirkcudbrightshire…'

The central character of *Other People's Rules* (2000) by **Julia Hamilton** (daughter of Lord Belhaven and Stenton, and brought up in Kirkcudbrightshire) is the Earl of Gatehouse – Lord Lieutenant of the Stewartry, Margaret Thatcher's agriculture spokesman in the House of Lords, a glamorous aristocrat much favoured by the tabloid gossip-columnists. He is also a serial seducer of teenage girls, including his own daughter, her schoolfriend, and the daughter of a pop star living on the estate next to Gatehouse Park. The last of these is killed and the Earl is charged with her murder. The trial, which takes place in Dumfries, is a media sensation:

> The rabble outside - there are many unemployed owing to the collapse of farming in the locality (you can buy a sheep for less than a packet of crisps at Wallets Marts [sic] in Castle Douglas) - seems mesmerized by the fact that Earl Gatehouse is on trial for this terrible killing. The proceedings are extensively reported every day in the national as well as the local press; there are American film crews from CNN and chic black-clad arty types chattering in French or Italian while they handle microphones and camera equipment. Dumfries, for about the only time in its entire history, is at the centre of the universe.

Before the scandal unfolds, one of the Earl's daughters comments on a swearing habit her sister Sarah has picked up at boarding-school:

> 'Your language!' said Louise admiringly. 'I think it's money down the drain, Pa, that posh school. You should have sent her to Kirkcudbright Academy.' This was a 1500-strong comprehensive in the county town a few miles from Gatehouse Park, described by Sarah even then as being full of girl gangs and lippy youths who all looked as if they had razor blades up their sleeves.

In a newspaper interview Julia Hamilton spoke of her estrangement from her father and confessed to having put him into the book. Lord Belhaven and Stenton appears as 'Lord Glengap' (a 'rather minor lord') along with 'his new Polish wife' (the author's stepmother is Polish). So much for the author's disclaimer: 'Any resemblance to actual persons…is entirely coincidental'.

189

The Novelists

In the twenty-first century the Stewartry was again featuring in crime fiction. New Galloway-based writer **Catriona McPherson** created 1920s 'society sleuth' Dandy Gilver, and in her debut tale *After the Armistice Ball* (2005) Dandy's investigation into a diamonds theft brings her to Kirkandrews near Borgue and to Gatehouse of Fleet:

> By the time we were on the coast road, coming round the bay to Kirkandrews in the failing afternoon light, I was even looking forward to it. A few days spent in this soft, fresh breeze…was a pleasant prospect. My debut as an investigator was almost too easy to be called employment.

But Dandy has her work cut out when she discovers that the Kirkandrews cottage where her investigation is to begin has just been destroyed by fire.

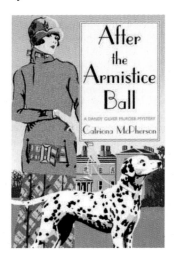

The Artists

Since the late-nineteenth century the Stewartry has enjoyed a reputation as a painters' paradise. They found all they wanted in the area: unspoilt scenery that yet was easily accessible by railway from the cities; a light that is said to be painter-friendly; and (until the more recent holiday-home boom) the availability of inexpensive living and studio space. Some one hundred and fifty artists are reckoned to have had an association with the area. Many of them settled there permanently, especially in Kirkcudbright, which as a result became known as an artists' colony and is today marketed by the heritage tourism industry as The Artists Town. But not all of the talent was incoming, and Kirkcudbright was not the only place where the talent flourished.

Nineteenth-century Gatehouse of Fleet got an early start as an artistic centre, and it all emanated from a single extraordinary family at Barlay Mill on the northern edge of the village. Of the six children born to James and Mary Faed, five went on to exhibit at the major British academies: John, James, Thomas, Susan and George. (The sixth, William, became a farmer in Australia).

Thomas Faed (1826-1900) was the most conspicuously successful of them all. His father was not keen on any of the children taking up such an insecure profession, so Thomas began his working life as an apprentice draper in Castle Douglas. After his father's death, he moved to Edinburgh where he began his formal art training. While still a student, he was exhibiting at the Royal Scottish Academy. By 1852 he was doing well enough to feel confident about moving to London. Financially, this

Thomas Faed

was the making of him. His sentimental renditions of themes from Scottish history and rural life - like *The Mitherless Bairn* and *The Last of the Clan* - were hugely popular and widely disseminated through reproductions. In 1864 he was made a Royal Academician.

John Faed (1819-1902) was the eldest and a mentor to his siblings. As a boy he was precociously adept at drawing and painting miniatures, which he would sell by raffle. He overcame his father's disapproval and went to Edinburgh where, just one year

after starting his studies, he had his first showing at the Royal Scottish Academy. He was elected to full membership of the RSA in 1851. Encouraged by the success of Thomas in London, he too decided to move south in 1864. Like his brother, he painted big narratives of Scottish rural life, many of them taking their inspiration from the novels of Sir Walter Scott and the poems of Robert Burns. He also depicted scenes from Shakespeare and the Bible.

But the call of Galloway was strong for John. After the death of his mother in 1866, he no longer had somewhere to stay during his regular return visits to Gatehouse. So the following year he bought a plot of land overlooking the village, and there his holiday home Ardmore, later to become a permanent residence, was built.

> After building our house at Gatehouse it was our habit of spending about six months of the year at Ardmore. This was done successively for 8 to 10 years, but, finding that the class of subjects I was then engaged with required country models, and Gatehouse could supply them of all ages, in perfection, I finally resolved to leave London, which I did in 1880.

James Faed (1821-1911), the second eldest, also migrated to Edinburgh, initially to study engineering, but John and Thomas encouraged him to take up engraving. He reproduced many of his brothers' images, and came to be regarded as one of the finest mezzotinters of his generation. Queen Victoria was an admirer, gave him numerous commissions and entertained him at Balmoral. He too had his London period but preferred Edinburgh, to which he returned in 1855 to remain for the rest of his life.

Susan Faed (1827-1909) had talent but no training. As the only daughter, it was she who inevitably had to stay at home to look after their mother when she was widowed; and later on, when John was left on his own, she kept house for him too. Nevertheless, she managed to get exhibited at the Academies in both Edinburgh and London. James said of her: 'Susan Faed painted some beautiful heads and would have risen to eminence if she had worked, but she would not work. It was always a marvel to me that she could do such things with studying so little'. When she married in her late fifties, he commented: 'she got married at last so painting ceased'.

The Cooran Lane, James Faed Jnr

George Faed (1830-52) was the youngest and shared James's talent for engraving. But a promising career was cut short by his early death from consumption.

The Faed genius lived on through the next generation: **James Faed Jnr** (1856-1920) was well-known for his heather landscapes; his younger brother **William Cotton Faed** (1858-1937), who ended up living in the Channel Islands, was a portraitist and landscapist; and Thomas's son **John Francis Faed** (1859-1904) specialised in seascapes.

E A Hornel memorial at Kirkcudbright Academy

Kirkcudbright's outstanding native talent was **Edward Atkinson Hornel** (1864-1933). Throughout his career he remained resolutely rooted in the town – yet achieved international renown, such that when in 1901 he was elected an Associate of the Royal Scottish Academy he felt able haughtily to reject the honour.

Although he was actually born in Australia, his parents were Kirkcudbright folk, and he was brought back home while still a toddler. After studying in both Edinburgh and Antwerp, he returned to Kirkcudbright in 1885 and set up his first studio behind the former Custom House at 21 High Street, across the road from the family home.

He became associated with the 'Glasgow Boys' group – Scotland's equivalent to the French Impressionists and Post-

Impressionists - and many of the friends he made in the art world, notably **James Guthrie** (1859-1930) and **David Gauld** (1865-1936), started regularly visiting Kirkcudbright.

Hornel's closest colleague in the early years was **George Henry** (1858-1943). Together they experimented with an exuberant style of painting in which representation was subservient to decoration. They became controversial figures.

One of Hornel's own paintings caused a furore in Liverpool when it was exhibited at the Walker Art Gallery in 1892. The municipal authorities were split over a proposal to acquire it for the permanent collection. The purchase went through only because the alderman behind the idea made it a resigning issue. *Summer* was the first 'Glasgow Boys' picture, apart from commissioned portraits, to be bought for a major public collection in the UK.

In 1893 Hornel and Henry went to Japan for an extended stay to investigate the reality behind the *fin de siècle* vogue for all things Eastern. They were away for 19 months. All but one of Hornel's Japanese paintings were sold when they went on show in Glasgow in 1895.

His success brought substantial financial rewards. In 1901 he bought the imposing eighteenth-century Broughton House at 12 High Street (now run by the National Trust for Scotland). He was particularly devoted to his garden, and, inspired by his visit to the Far East, incorporated Japanese motifs into its design.

A characteristic later Hornel (National Trust for Scotland)

Hornel was also very interested in the history of Galloway, and had a special fascination for the prehistoric cup-and-ring rock carvings to be found in the vicinity. In 1919 he began collecting old Galloway books, and also anything to do with Robert Burns. His library eventually consisted of some 15,000 volumes.

He fully participated in the affairs of the town, serving on the town council, though later resigning over a now obscure row about pavements. He chaired the local Decorations Committee for Queen Victoria's Diamond Jubilee celebrations, and advised on the design of the town's War Memorial. In his later years he was on the bench as an Honorary Sheriff. His civic duties became increasingly focused on education: for three years he was on the county's education committee, and he conducted the negotiations with an American philanthropist which resulted in the building of a gymnasium for Kirkcudbright Academy.

His early artistic radicalism gave way to an easy and lucrative formula of pretty seashore and woodland scenes with young girls (based on locals) cavorting around. In his studio work he relied more and more on photographs. When he painted outdoors – for example, at Brighouse Bay, where he had a hut for summer use – he was driven to the location by his chauffeur.

Hornel never married. Until his death in 1933, he shared Broughton House with his sister Elizabeth ('Tizzie').

As well as Gatehouse of Fleet's star returnee John Faed, Hornel in his early days had other artistic comrades in the native pool of talent in the Stewartry. **Thomas Bromley Blacklock** (1863-1903) was a fine landscape artist until, depressed by chronic ill-health, he committed suicide. Castle Douglas's **William Stewart MacGeorge** (1861-1931), with whom Hornel had been at college, spent much of his time in Kirkcudbright before eventually settling in East Lothian. **William Mouncey** (1852-1901), who married one of Hornel's sisters, was a local house-painter who went on to make his name as a painter of pictures. In nearby Dundrennan, there was **John Copland** (1854-1929), not only a landscape painter but also a pioneering photographer.

It was, however, the steady migration into Kirkcudbright of professional artists from other parts of the country that turned the town into the 'St Ives of Scotland'. Undoubtedly, the presence of Hornel, famous and well-connected in artistic circles throughout Scotland, had a magnetic effect. Among the early arrivals were **William Robson** (1863-1950), a dazzling pastellist and one-time chairman of the Society of Scottish Artists who became legendary for the weekly parties he hosted for fellow artists at 50 High Street, and **Charles Oppenheimer** (1875-1961) who re-located from Manchester in 1908, becoming Hornel's next-door neighbour.

The Art Nouveau virtuoso **Jessie Marion King** (1875-1949) and her 'Glasgow Style' all-rounder husband **Ernest Archibald Taylor** (1874-1951) took up permanent residence in Kirkcudbright in 1914, turning 46 High Street into the now iconic Greengate. Around the same time **William Hanna Clarke** (1882-1924) gave up dentistry in Glasgow to pursue his dream of being a full-time artist but he died tragically early following an accident.

The extraordinary partnership of King and Taylor attracted another wave of settlers, many of whom lived in the cottages the Taylors had renovated for rental in the Greengate Close. **Anna Hotchkis** (1885-1984), best known for work based on her daring travels through remote China in the 1920s, came to the town as a young graduate and was still there when she died weeks away from her centenary. An influential tutor at Edinburgh College of Art used to tell his students that their education would be complete only after a period with the Taylors in Kirkcudbright.

Throughout the 1920s and '30s there was a steady flow of new settlers: Royal Scottish Academy stalwarts **Robert Sivell** (1888-1958) and **John Charles Lamont** (1894-1948), two friends who married local sisters; the Old Etonian gentleman-artist **David Sassoon** (1888-1978); and 'Glasgow Boys' veteran **Robert Macaulay Stevenson** (1854-1952). Some, like the great Scottish Colourist **Samuel John Peploe** (1871-1935) came for extended stays rather than settling permanently. As a regular visitor to the Stewartry throughout the 1920s, the writer **Dorothy L Sayers** came to know the Kirkcudbright artists well and immortalised them in her Lord Peter Wimsey novel of 1931, *Five Red Herrings* (see The Novelists).

The Second World War brought another influx. The eminent animal portraitist **William Miles Johnston** (1893-1974) and his wife **Dorothy Nesbitt** (1893-1974) supplemented their earnings by running a shop called The Crafts at 15 Castle Street, while at 17 Castle Street their friend **Lena Alexander** (1899-1983) showed similar initiative with her ladies' clothes shop, Alexis. Wartime also brought

Typical Stewartry scene by William Miles Johnston

Thomas Lochhead giving a potting demonstration

Jankel Adler (1895-1949), a Jewish refugee from Poland, and the famous cartoonist **Ronald Searle** (born 1920), whose hugely popular St Trinian's School cartoons were inspired by his experiences in Kirkcudbright.

The final inflow into the original artists' colony (as opposed to today's Artists Town) came after the Second World War: the immensely well-connected painter **Cecile Walton** (1891-1956), daughter of the 'Glasgow Boy' E A Walton; the sculptor **Phyllis Bone** (1896-1972), the first woman to be elected to the Royal Scottish Academy; the pioneering potter **Thomas Lochhead** (1917-2005); and the couthie artistic jack-of-all-trades **Tim Jeffs** (1904-1975).

There were many more artists, both settlers and long-stay visitors, too many to mention (the full story can be found in the present author's *Tales of the Kirkcudbright Artists*). They enriched the community by fully participating in its day-to-day life. William Robson crewed on the Kirkcudbright lifeboat and ran the town's football team. Jessie King designed for local pageants and plays and, if asked, would decorate any child's hard-boiled egg at Easter. William Miles Johnston and Lena Alexander helped drama and operatic societies with costumes and make-up. Dorothy Nesbitt did service in local government and was central to saving the dilapidated riverside property that would later be turned into the Harbour Cottage Gallery. Cecile Walton ran the Kirkcudbright Children's Theatre.

It was not just dramatic talent that Walton was good at spotting. She was responsible for discovering the artistic potential of local schoolboy **John Halliday** (born 1933), overcoming the obstacles to his entering Glasgow School of Art and thereby sending him off on the road to becoming the most accomplished *native* Kirkcudbright painter since Hornel. As a youngster in the 1940s, Halliday knew many of the famous colonists in addition to Walton, and his career has been a living link with an artistic phenomenon which had otherwise effectively petered out by the early 1960s.

The 'granite town' of Dalbeattie had no artists' colony like Kirkcudbright's, but in the twentieth century it did produce two interesting painters, one of national stature, the other a one-off character of local renown.

John Maxwell (1905-1962) was born and died in the town (where his father ran the cinema for a time) and, although his teaching career took him away some of the time, he always regarded himself as being based primarily in Dalbeattie at the family home Millbrooke, where he added a skylight to an upstairs bedroom so that it could be used as a studio.

After Edinburgh College of Art, he studied at the Academie Moderne in Paris, followed by a year in Spain and Italy. One of his Paris tutors was the Cubist-inclined Fernand Leger, but Maxwell's own preferences were towards the Symbolism of Odilon Redon and the mysticism of Marc Chagall. His closest involvement remained with Edinburgh College of Art: he

View From A Tent, John Maxwell

returned as a teacher for various periods until the year before his death. Fellow student William Gillies became a lifelong friend, and the two of them went travelling and painting together, including to the Stewartry, and held joint exhibitions.

Maxwell first exhibited at the Royal Scottish Academy in 1937, and was elected to full RSA membership in 1949. He was notoriously self-critical. It is said that on one occasion he was on a bus from Dalbeattie to Edinburgh to get eight watercolours framed but decided during the journey to destroy six of them. A year after his death the Scottish National Gallery of Modern Art in Edinburgh held a memorial exhibition: there were 150 works.

John Maxwell's presence in Dalbeattie had an inspirational effect on a local man who, despite never having had a formal training, eventually fulfilled his longing to make a living from painting. The unmistakably idiosyncratic landscapes of **Jim Sturgeon** (1932-2006) earned him the title 'The Galloway Colourist'. Maxwell saw his early efforts and encouraged him. So too did the Glasgow-based painter Donald Bain, follower of the Scottish Colourists, whose advice to Jim was: 'Have a bash and do what pleases you and you only... Don't worry about perspective, accuracy has nothing to do with

The Wee Jetty, Kippford, Jim Sturgeon

art, it is stock-in-trade of technicians and precision engineers.'

Jim finally went full-time in 1967 and through all the vicissitudes of a precarious profession stuck at it to the end. Two years before he died, a stroke robbed him of the use of his right hand, so he learned to paint with his left.

For over half a century St John's Town of Dalry in the Glenkens was home for the eminent wildlife artist **Donald Watson** (1918-2005). Watson's special interest was birds, and his quality lay in being not only artistically gifted but also an ornithological expert.

His enthusiasm began early in life. During a childhood spent at Cranleigh in Surrey, he had the privilege of meeting and being encouraged by the famous wildlife illustrator Archibald Thorburn. He found more mentors when, after his father's death, his mother moved the family to Edinburgh, where he attended Edinburgh Academy, followed by a history degree at St John's College in Oxford. After service in the Second World War, a patron encouraged him to work in Dumfriesshire – this set him on a professional path, and also introduced him to the ornithological delights of south-west Scotland. He and his wife settled in Dalry in 1951.

In the early 1960s he embarked upon his first major publishing commission. He spent two years producing 96 colour plates for the *Oxford Book of British Birds.* Many more commissions followed – not just as illustrator but as writer too, as in *Birds of Moor and Mountain* (1972). *The Hen Harrier* (1977), about the species that most fascinated him, is now accepted as a classic. In later life there were volumes of a more autobiographical bent: *A Bird Artist in Scotland* (1988) and *One Pair of Eyes* (1994), the latter title having a particular poignancy because he was by then beginning to lose his sight.

The Artists

From artists to architects: many of the prestigious buildings of the Stewartry were designed by fashionable city-based architects like the Adam brothers and David Bryce. There were few distinguished locally based architects. The most prolific of them was **Walter Newall** (1780-1863). The son of a New Abbey farmer, Newall began as a furniture designer in Dumfries and progressed into civil engineering and architecture. He was a beneficiary of the boom in kirk building that took place in the first half of the nineteenth century. His first commission was for Buittle kirk (1819), and his other Stewartry ecclesiastical credits include the kirks at Lochrutton (1819), Anwoth (1827), Parton (1833) and Kirkpatrick Durham (1850). His style is recognisable: his kirks usually have a square tower at the end with four spiky pinnacles on top.

He also designed large country houses, among them Dildawn near Bridge of Dee (1813), Kilquhanity (1820s) near Kirkpatrick Durham and Glenlair (1830s) near Corsock. He was responsible for the upgrading of numerous other buildings, for example Spottes Hall at Haugh of Urr and the kirk at Kirkbean.

In music **Cecil Coles** (1888-1918) is the closest the Stewartry can come to claiming to have nurtured a famous composer, though in this case the fame did not come until 80 years after his death.

Coles, son of the artist and archaeologist Frederick Coles, was born and brought up in Kirkcudbright. The family later moved to Edinburgh, where Coles completed his education at George Watson's School before proceeding to the London School of Music, where he befriended Gustav Holst.

Coles was a stretcher-bearer in the First World War. In April 1918, just months before the end of the conflict, he was carrying a casualty when he himself was shot dead by a sniper. His military gravestone in northern France quotes Holst: 'He was a genius before anything else and a hero of the first water'.

His manuscripts were stored at George Watson's. It was only in the 1990s that his daughter discovered the existence of the archive, and this led to the first recording of his work in 2002, including the poignant orchestral suite *Behind the Lines*, which he had started in the trenches but never lived to finish.

The Movie

The Stewartry has become a place of pilgrimage for fans of the 1970s movie *The Wicker Man,* which was shot partly in the county. Cheaply and chaotically made, with a demoralised crew and unhappy stars, this film ought to have disappeared irrecoverably into the archive. But its theme of pagan eroticism continues to appeal to adherents of 'alternative' lifestyles, many of whom make an annual trek to The Wickerman Festival, a rock-music event that every July turns a farm near Dundrennan into the Stewartry's own wee version of Glastonbury.

Apart from a few scenes shot in Kirkcudbright and Gatehouse of Fleet, the two principal locations within the county were Anwoth and Creetown. A ritualistic dance is performed within the ruins of Anwoth Old Kirk; while the interiors of the film's Green Man pub are those of the Ellangowan Hotel in Creetown. Summerisle, the story's fictional setting, was meant to be in the Hebrides off the north-west coast of Scotland, but in fact the film was shot entirely on the Scottish mainland.

The season is supposed to be spring, but it was the late autumn/early winter of 1972 when they were shooting in the Stewartry. Artificial blossom had to be added to the bare winter trees. The weather at the time was damp and cold, one reason for the miserable mood that descended upon the cast, which included Edward Woodward, Christopher Lee, Diane Cilento and Britt Ekland.

Scene from *The Wicker Man*

The Movie

Ekland was the most miserable of them all. Almost none of her colleagues knew at the time that she had just discovered she was pregnant by her then boyfriend. In the absence of the boyfriend, she felt alone and anxious. She did not enjoy staying at the Kirroughtree Hotel near Newton Stewart, where she had to use a shared bathroom, and she was not impressed by Newton Stewart. In an interview with a Sunday newspaper, she described the place as being full of hardened drinkers: it 'had to be the most dismal place in Creation...one of the bleakest places I've been to in my life'. The publication of her views caused a local furore. Through the *Galloway Gazette,* the town's provost hit back: 'She comes from Sweden and what are they noted for? Illegitimacy, promiscuity and permissiveness'. As for drink, the provost added: 'I saw Miss Ekland at various functions. She seemed capable of downing great quantities of drink'.

The film's producer was forced to issue a conciliatory statement:

> Any goosepimples which our Sassenach skins suffered during our stay with you were quickly smoothed away by the warmth of our personal relationships with you. I would like to dissociate all of us from the comments made by Miss Ekland and I hope you will accept my own personal apology.

Ekland had been cast, more for her looks than for her acting ability, as Willow MacGregor, the sexy daughter of the Green Man's landlord. Her strong Swedish accent was a considerable

obstacle. In a later dubbing session, she attempted to re-do her dialogue with a Scottish accent. But the result was embarrassingly bad, and, without Ekland's knowledge and to her later dismay, the Scottish actress and jazz singer Annie Ross was brought in during post-production to do the final version of Willow's voice.

Not only do we not hear Ekland's voice - it is not entirely her body we see in the famous nude scene. 'She was perfectly prepared to show her tits', the director Robin Hardy explained years later, 'but we had to get a night-club go-go dancer very quickly to play her backside.'

Britt Ekland as Willow

202

Other Pairs of Eyes

C elebrity travellers of the past, heading from the south into Scotland, have in so many cases gone straight for the Highlands and Islands in search of the picturesque. However, some had the good fortune, after crossing the border, to turn westwards and thereby discover the Stewartry, Scotland's 'best-kept secret'.

John Macky, whose *A Journey through Scotland* was published in 1723, noted how different the people were from the English:

> The common people wear all bonnets instead of hats; and though some of the townsmen have hats, they wear them only on Sundays and extraordinary occasions. There is nothing of the gaiety of the English, but a sedate gravity in every face, without the stiffness of the Spanish; and I take this to be owing to their praying, and frequent long graces, which gives their looks a religious cast.

He was not impressed by his lodgings in Kirkcudbright ('the room where I lay, I believe, had not been washed in a hundred years') and he was disappointed to discover that there would be no Sunday roast dinner because it was the Sabbath. He would have to wait for a late supper after church:

> Certainly no nation on earth observes the Sabbath with that strictness of devotion and resignation to the will of God; they all pray in their families before they go to church, and between sermons they fast. After sermon every body retires to his own home and reads some book of devotion till supper, which is generally very good on Sundays, after which they sing psalms till they go to bed.

Daniel Defoe, author of *Robinson Crusoe*, was sent to Scotland prior to the 1707 union with England to report on conditions. He claimed to have found the port of Kirkcudbright moribund:

> Here is a pleasant situation, and yet nothing pleasant to be seen. Here is a harbour without ships, a port without trade, a fishery without nets, a people without business; and, that which is worse than all, they do not seem to desire business, much less do they understand it...though here is an extraordinary salmon fishing, the salmon come and offer themselves, and go again, and cannot obtain the privilege of being made useful to mankind; for they take very few of them.

Other Pairs of Eyes

Wherever he went in the Stewartry, Defoe saw poverty:

> ...the common people all over this country, not only are poor, but look poor; they appear dejected and discouraged, as if they had given over all hopes of ever being otherwise than what they are.

 The English poet **John Keats** crossed the Stewartry with his friend Charles Brown during their walking-tour of 1818. Three years earlier Sir Walter Scott's novel *Guy Mannering*, with its gypsy character Meg Merrilies, had been published. 'We are in the midst of Meg Merrilies' country,' Keats wrote to his sister, enclosing the poem he had just composed:

> Old Meg she was a gypsey,
> And liv'd upon the moors
> Her bed it was the brown heath turf
> And her house was out of doors
>
> Her apples were swart blackberries
> Her currants pods o' broom
> Her wine was dew o' the wild white rose
> Her book a churchyard tomb...

Keats described Kirkcudbrightshire as: 'very beautiful, very wild with craggy hills somewhat in the westmoreland fashion...very fine with a little of Devon.' Yet he clearly felt he was in another country:

> Our landlady of yesterday said very few Southrens passed these ways. The children jabber away as in a foreign language. We dined yesterday on dirty bacon, dirtier eggs and dirtiest potatoes with a slice of salmon. We drink water for dinner diluted with a gill of whiskey.

Like many other visitors, Keats claimed to see the harm caused by strict religion: 'A Scotch girl stands in terrible awe of the Elders – poor little Susannas – They will scarcely laugh – they are greatly to be pitied and the Kirk is greatly to be damn'd.' His companion Charles Brown (whose father was Scottish) reported:

> Keats has been these five hours abusing the Scotch and their country. He says that the women have large splay feet, which is too true to be controverted, and that he thanks Providence he is not related to a Scot, nor in any way connected with them.

Henry, Lord Cockburn (1779-1854) was an acerbic chronicler of his journeys around Scotland as a circuit judge. In 1839 he entered the Stewartry by way of the coast road from New Abbey to Colvend:

> I had been told (but only by Galwegians) to expect something uncommonly fine along this part of the shores of the Solway, and from this highway. I was disappointed. It is the stupidest of all our Firths. Few rocks, no islands, and especially no edging of picturesque mountains. For to point, as the natives always do, to the dim ghosts of some distant hills, of which only the outlines are visible, and to explain, with an air of triumph, these are the English mountains, is mere stuff. They are too far off to be felt as parts of the real picture.

In 1844 Cockburn was travelling along the coast road at the opposite end of the Stewartry, passing Creetown and heading for Newton Stewart, and again had something to complain of:

> Creetown and Newton-Stewart are beautifully situated, and seen at a little distance amidst their sheltering trees, look like capitals in Arcadia; but oh, oh! when they are entered!! Not even the peat-flavoured air — whispering the approach of a Highland village so agreeably — can save them. Styes for human swine.

From his lodgings at Cumstoun on the outskirts of Kirkcudbright, he climbed to the top of Tongland Hill for its classic view of the town. His admiration was less than total:

> I doubt if there be a more picturesque country town in Scotland. Small, clean, silent, and respectable; it seems (subject, however, to one enormous deduction) the type of place to which decent characters and moderate purses would retire for quiet comfort. The deduction arises from the dismal swamps of deep, sleechy mud, by which it is nearly surrounded at low tide. It is a dreadful composition... Think of being surrounded by a dirty substance, impossible to be touched, and most dangerous to be gone upon. A town surrounded by a lake of bird-lime!

But his verdict when the tide was in: 'From several aspects it is the Venice of Scotland!'

The indefatigable literary walker **George Borrow**, author of *Lavengro* and *Wild Wales*, passed through the Stewartry in 1866.

He left only the sketchiest of notes, the most entertaining being about suffering the effects of Sabbatarianism. On a very hot day, 'gasping with heat' somewhere between Gatehouse of Fleet and Kirkcudbright, he entered an inn in search of refreshment but was turned away – 'We dinna sell onything on a Sunday'.

Around 1930 the legendary Scots music-hall entertainer **Sir Harry Lauder** came to the south-west of Scotland for a holiday. He told a local newspaper reporter:

> Galloway takes some beatin'. I've telt folks that; it's a gran' corner o' Scotland. Ye hae every kin' o' scenery. It's a dreamland down here. Why don't ye advertise it? Tell the world about Galloway.

Lauder went on a car tour of the region, observed by local author Andrew McCormick. After lunch at a hotel in Carsphairn, they emerged to discover a crowd of people taking photographs. Lauder had earlier been spotted by a woman who had performed with him many years previously, and word of his presence had passed swiftly around the village:

> While the crowd photographed Sir Harry and his friends, the friends retaliated by photographing the crowd. The depth of hero-worship was reached when Sir Harry lit his pipe and flung down the match, and a youthful admirer stepped behind him and took possession of it! As Sir Harry renewed his acquaintance with the lady who had known him in his early days, the crowd sang songs. The lady led the company in singing 'Keep right on to the end of the road', and as the motor moved away, they sang, 'Will ye no' come back again', out of gratitude to Sir Harry for the pleasure he had often given to them, and for the happy way in which he had allowed himself to be photographed as a souvenir of that memorable meeting and ovation which had sprung up as quietly as a summer breeze.

J J Bell, best known for his *Wee MacGreegor*, travelled through the Stewartry in the early 1930s for his travel book *The Glory of Scotland* (1932). He was moved by the proliferation of hillside memorials to the Covenanting 'martyrs' who died fighting against Episcopalianism:

> To some of us the Covenanters, with all respect to their

206

courage, may appear as stiff-necked and aggravating psalm-singing people, while the dragoons did only their duty; to others the dragoons' was a foul duty, while the Covenanters stood for Scottish freedom, as surely as did Wallace and Bruce. So we might argue within four walls, out of the abundance of our bookish knowledge; but at the graves in those lonely open spaces the tragedy comes close, so close that we see the blood on the heather and hear the weeping of those who have stolen back to see their beloved dead...

Bell cheered up when he arrived in Kirkcudbright:

> Kirkcudbright, beloved of artists, is sweetly set on the Dee, a few miles from the Solway Firth. It is the sort of country town that one likes at first sight - quiet, roomy, wholesome, mainly modern, yet fortunate in the survival of ancient land-marks in its very midst.

The Stewartry was by-passed by the great travel writer **H V Morton** in his classic *In Search of Scotland*, but got fulsome treat-ment in the sequel *In Scotland Again* (1933). Everything about the area seduced him:

> The fields slope up towards queer, nibbled-looking hills which grow the greenest grass I have ever seen. They are low, fairy-like hills. If they were in Donegal you would swear that there were leprechauns in them. There is an air of enchantment over them. They look as though they might open and let loose into the world something that has been sleeping for centuries beneath the heather.

Morton arrived at Kirkcudbright late at night in a violent storm. 'Seldom have I seen a more sinister building,' he wrote of his first glimpse of the Tolbooth in darkness. However:

> In the morning, what a change: I looked out on an irre-proachable Scottish town. There was a row of whitewashed houses, a milkman going his rounds, and at the end of the street was the Tolbooth, looking almost friendly in the morning sun.
>
> Kirkcudbright is one of the most picturesque and fasci-nating Lowland towns I have seen. I think if I wanted to send a stranger to a town which expresses its locality as definitely as county towns in England express their coun-ties, I would send him to the capital of the Stewartry.

The town is good-looking. It is small enough to be interesting and not small enough to be boring. Every one knows every one else's business, his relatives, his virtues and his vices; and so Kirkcudbright teems with human interest.

 Around the same time the Scottish poet **Edwin Muir**, who spent most of his adult life out of Scotland, returned for a grand tour of his native land for his *Scottish Journey* (1935). As he crossed the Nith westwards and entered the Stewartry, he was immediately impressed by the character of the landscape:

Dumfriesshire is mainly rolling country, mounting and falling in wide, easy sweeps. But in Kirkcudbrightshire the ground is delicately varied, and the small abrupt hills are broken up into little terraced shelves of green. This interruption of all the contours arrests the eye perpetually; there are no grand effects; everything is plain and exquisite. The trees are not massed in thick woods as in Dumfriesshire, but distributed singly or in little clumps, as in a free and open design. So just and classical are the natural contours that a group of cows planted on an abrupt green hill seemed, as I looked, to improvise a sort of rustic Acropolis and Parthenon all complete.

Muir was less impressed by the people:

I reached Kirkcudbright, hot and covered with dust. I stopped at the first hotel I saw and asked if I could have a room for the night. The hotel proprietor first gave me a look, then went to the door, gave a look at the car too, seemed to hesitate for a moment, but then said yes, I could have a room.

After dinner, during which he was irritated by a party of noisy English tourists, he went for a walk along the High Street where he saw 'many quaint and charming houses', but also…

…a fat strong gypsy-like woman in beach pyjamas who was swearing volubly at a little pale-faced boy, probably her son or step-son, who was crouching on the steps of a house. All the acrid and devastating energy of the Scottish character seemed to be in the harridan's voice; her words were like actual missiles shot from her mouth, for the wretched boy jerked and trembled perpetually under them. Yet I doubt whether there was hatred or even anger in them; they had an almost objective sound, as if they were a mere discharge of energy, enjoyable in itself, and without colour or inflection. The sound of them brought back to me many an hour in Glasgow, where long before I had suffered in a less disagreeable way from the distorted, incessant and yet purposeless energy broadcast by the people I met.

Resuming his walk, Muir again found something to be annoyed about:

Presently I found myself at a gate leading into a field ad-joining the river, and asked two men, who were also dark and gypsy-like like the woman, and by their appearance seemed to be fishermen, if the path would take me down to the sea. They stopped their conversation and looked at me for a minute, then one of them said in a reluctant voice: 'Ay, ye *could* get to the sea that way,' his words seeming to imply that there were other and more usual routes. But, having given me an exact answer, he did not seem to think there was any necessity to embroider it with explanations, and turning to his companion resumed his talk.

It is small wonder that Muir's publisher warned on the dust-jacket: 'No reader thinking to find the Scotland of the tourist's de-light should open this book'!

In 1986 **Richard West** visited Kirkcudbright for *The Spectator* magazine:

...Kirkcudbright seems to have stayed clear of most con-temporary nonsense. An Englishman, who has settled here after the army, said to me: 'I took one look at Kirkcudbright and saw that it wasn't in the twentieth century...

West's visit revived a memory for him:

Many years ago, someone told me of having visited here and seen on the wall of a public gents this plaintive appeal: 'Is there not one queer in Kirkcudbright?'

A jaundiced account of the Stewartry came at the start of the twenty-first century from the London-based journalist **Charles Jennings** in *Faintheart: An Englishman Ventures North of the Bor-der* (2001). His powers of observation cannot be entirely trusted, since he mis-spells Kirkcudbright and in the following passage appears to have mistaken a creamery for a power station:

A furtive detour took me through Kircudbright [sic] and some standard roughcast hutches, until I found the centre of town. This turned out to be an artists' community. Many of the trad stone Scottish houses had been painted in blithe Mediterranean colours and offered B&B just as if we were in the West Country. There were shops selling free-range daubs and modellings and there was a restaurant called Artie's to rub the point home. There was even a bloke posing as an artist by standing on the edge of the pavement, wearing black jeans, a black leather drape jacket and a white collarless shirt and goatee…

The whole thing was saved from its own extravagant pretensions, though, by the presence of a nice big centrally sited warehouse for builders' skips immediately opposite the dieselly Texaco garage. These chimed in with a stupidly hideous bridge over the River Dee and, in the distance, a looming hydro-electric plant like a Church of Divine Ugliness. Seven out of ten, in other words.

Haste ye back, Mr Jennings.

One legendary writer of the twentieth century who actually lived in the Stewartry for a time has left no account of his sojourn. That is not surprising, since **T E Lawrence** ('Lawrence of Arabia') was only one-year-old in 1889 when his parents brought him to live at 89 St Mary Street in Kirkcudbright. His father was a titled Irishman who ran off with the family governess. The couple assumed the identity of 'Mr and Mrs Lawrence' as they led a peripatetic existence before finally settling in Oxford. Kirkcudbright was a two-year stopover in their wanderings. T E Lawrence's younger brother William was born in the town. There is no evidence that the author of *The Seven Pillars of Wisdom* (1926) ever re-visited this scene of his early childhood.

Index

Index

212

Index

Index

Index